GOD'S GIRL AND FRIENDSHIP

FOR GIRLS LIKE YOU

HARVEST Kids

HARVEST HOUSE PUBLISHERS
EUGENE, OREGON

Written by Linsey Driskill with contributions from
Alena Pitts Franklin, Kaitlyn Pitts, Camryn Pitts, and Olivia Pitts

Unless otherwise indicated, all Scripture verses are taken from the Holy Bible, New International Version®, NIV®. Copyright © 1973, 1978, 1984, 2011 by Biblica, Inc. Used with permission of Zondervan. All rights reserved worldwide. www.zondervan.com.

Verses marked HCSB are taken from the Holman Christian Standard Bible®, Copyright © 1999, 2000, 2002, 2003, 2009 by Holman Bible Publishers. Used with permission. Holman Christian Standard Bible®, Holman CSB®, and HCSB® are federally registered trademarks of Holman Bible Publishers.

Verses marked ESV are taken from the ESV® Bible (The Holy Bible, English Standard Version®), copyright © 2001 by Crossway, a publishing ministry of Good News Publishers. Used with permission. All rights reserved. The ESV text may not be quoted in any publication made available to the public by a Creative Commons license. The ESV may not be translated in whole or in part into any other language.

Verses marked NLT are taken from the Holy Bible, New Living Translation, copyright © 1996, 2004, 2015 by Tyndale House Foundation. Used with permission of Tyndale House Publishers, Carol Stream, Illinois 60188. All rights reserved.

Cover design by Emily Weigel Design
Interior design by Angie Renich, Wildwood Digital Publishing
Cover and interior images © TashaNatasha / Shutterstock; LINECTOR, Natsicha, devitaayu, Saiful / Adobe Stock

For bulk, special sales, or ministry purchases, please call 1-800-547-8979.
Email: CustomerService@hhpbooks.com

This logo is a federally registered trademark of the Hawkins Children's LLC.
Harvest House Publishers, Inc., is the exclusive licensee of this trademark.

God's Girl and Friendship

Copyright © 2026 by For Girls Like You
Published by Harvest House Publishers
Eugene, Oregon 97408
www.harvesthousepublishers.com

ISBN 978-0-7369-9258-9 (pbk)
ISBN 978-0-7369-9259-6 (eBook)

Library of Congress Control Number: 2025944969

Printed in the United States of America

25 26 27 28 29 30 31 32 33 34 / VP / 10 9 8 7 6 5 4 3 2 1

Contents

Hey, girl, it's Alena—a fellow God's Girl.

If you're anything like me, you've probably got a lot of questions. About God, about life, about the world we live in...

There's so much we don't naturally understand, and the truth is, we all need a guide—someone to answer our deepest questions. The best part? We've already got one.

God, our maker who intentionally crafted each of us together, is our greatest guide. He is our help and leader. Without Him, we're like blind sheep just roaming through life.

We've been given all the tools we need to live out this thing we call life. Through God's Word, His Spirit inside of us, and community, we can trust that He is guiding us.

Community is where we come in.

We were created to walk with others. Asking questions and learning from those a few steps ahead of us is essential to the Christian walk. What you are holding in your hand— this guide—will offer some voices, insights, and answers, emphasizing the Word of God and helping you understand.

We can't know everything, but we can know some things! Buckle up for a fun adventure of learning as we go through life.

Introduction

Hey, girl!

This book is all about friendship. God made us for friendship. He made us to be in community—to love and to be loved. Because we are all imperfect, we have to work at our friendships to develop good, godly ones. You might be wondering...

How do I even make a friend?

How do I have good, close friendships?

What does a godly friendship look like?

So many girls have these same questions! You're not alone. In this book, you will learn about qualities that develop good friendships. For each quality, there is a **Soul Scripture** that connects with the quality, as well as a section called **Snapshot** that summarizes it.

To understand a word further, it is helpful to know its opposite meaning, or **Flipside**, which is the next section. In the **Unwind Your Mind** section, you can reflect on the quality in your journal. Journaling is a way to settle these truths deep into your heart by reflecting on them.

Last, in the **What Do I Do?** section, there are questions girls like you have about friendship. You might be able to relate to them. Our team members at For Girls Like You have answered them: Linsey Driskill, Alena Pitts Franklin, and Alena's sisters, Kaitlyn, Camryn, and Olivia.

Our hope and prayer is that through this friendship book, your understanding of healthy, good friendships would grow along with the friendships in your life. We hope you will know that you are deeply loved by God and He has great purposes for you.

QUALITIES
of
FRIENDSHIPS

Honesty

Soul Scripture

"A lying tongue hates those it hurts,
and a flattering mouth works ruin."
Proverbs 26:28

Snapshot

When someone is honest, you can trust them. Honesty holds friendships together. In Proverbs 26:28, how does a lying tongue feel about the person it hurts?

a) A lying tongue loves the person.

b) A lying tongue hates the person.

c) A lying tongue likes the person.

The verse also says, "A flattering mouth works _____."

These are strong words, but God is saying that lying and being dishonest hurts people and friendships. When we are honest, we are loving others. Think about it: If someone has lied to you, did you feel loved or hurt?

The second part of Proverbs 26:28 talks about flattery. Flattery is when someone says really nice things even when they don't mean it, usually because they think it is what people want to hear. An example of flattery is if someone tells a friend that she loves her outfit (even if she really thinks it's ugly) because she wants that person to like her.

Or flattery could be when a person agrees with everything a friend says (even if she thinks it's wrong or she disagrees) because she wants the friend to like her.

Honesty doesn't mean that every time you don't like an outfit or something a friend is doing you have to tell her. But if she asks you, you can be honest with kindness.

For example, how can you be a friend who is both honest and kind when someone tries on a new sweater and you think it's really ugly? Which option would be best?

a) Use flattery and tell her the sweater is beautiful on her.

b) Tell her it is the ugliest sweater you have ever seen and it would look better on a rhinoceros.

c) Tell her that you like the other sweaters better on her.

You can tell the person the truth, but with kindness! So *c* would definitely be the best answer. If a friend asks you a question, it's okay to have a different opinion—just be respectful.

Flipside

The flipside of honesty is dishonesty. In Luke 19, a dishonest man named Zacchaeus was a tax collector. He cheated, lied, and stole from people, so they couldn't stand him.

Why do you think people didn't want to be friends with Zacchaeus?

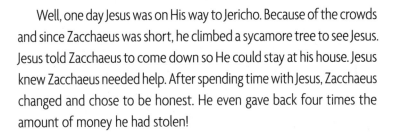

a) He was short.

b) He was dishonest.

c) His name began with Z.

Well, one day Jesus was on His way to Jericho. Because of the crowds and since Zacchaeus was short, he climbed a sycamore tree to see Jesus. Jesus told Zacchaeus to come down so He could stay at his house. Jesus knew Zacchaeus needed help. After spending time with Jesus, Zacchaeus changed and chose to be honest. He even gave back four times the amount of money he had stolen!

> Jesus said to [Zacchaeus], "Today salvation has come to this house, because this man, too, is a son of Abraham. For the Son of Man came to seek and to save the lost" (Luke 19:9-10).

What do you think helped Zacchaeus become honest?

a) He ate some great spaghetti and meatballs for dinner.

b) He was given a lie detector test.

c) He spent time with Jesus.

We can always come to Jesus and be forgiven and changed—just like Zacchaeus changed and became an honest person. Zacchaeus could finally start having good friendships since he started being honest. And we can too.

Honesty is an important part of good friendships.

Unwind Your Mind

? Do you think people liked Zacchaeus after he decided to be honest? Why?

_____

_____

_____

_____

_____

? Are you honest in your friendships? If not, how can you be more honest?

_____

_____

_____

_____

_____

What Do I Do?

"How can I be honest with my friend if I think she's making a bad decision?"

—Caroline

Dear Caroline,

This can be tough! When you see your friend making a hurtful decision, the easy way out is to be quiet and not say anything. But it ends up being more difficult to not say anything. Guilt can creep in when we know we should have spoken up.

Proverbs 27:6 says, "Wounds from a friend can be trusted, but an enemy multiplies kisses."

That means if you approve of everything a friend says and does, even if it's the wrong thing, you are really acting like an enemy to her. Outwardly, you agree with everything she is doing, but inwardly, you know your friend's choice is wrong.

If you tell your friend in a loving way that her choice might hurt herself and others, your honesty could create a wound at first, because sometimes the truth hurts. Even so, you are being a true friend because you are looking out for her heart.

Here's a helpful way to approach the conversation:

1. First, let your friend know that you care about her.

2. Tell her that is why you are being honest with her.

3. Let her know why you think her decision could be hurtful.

4. And then let her know that you are there for her.

Be a friend who cares enough to be honest. We're rooting you on, Caroline!

Love, For Girls Like You

> "How do I come clean with a friend if I have not been honest?"
>
> —Cate

Dear Cate,

Oh, this is a good one. If you have been dishonest with a friend, you're not alone. We all mess up from time to time. Because you asked this question, great job. You're already on the right track. We know that lying is a sin, and it's not how God wants us to live our lives. Thankfully, He's provided a way out.

Oftentimes, the reason we are dishonest is because we are afraid of what someone might think about us. We aim to please, and our friends' disapproval of us can feel scary and humiliating. However, honesty plays an important role in honoring our friends and our God. Making things right is the only way to preserve friendship.

First, you must confess. You should always confess to God first, knowing that your sin breaks His heart more than anyone else's. Embrace His forgiveness, and then go boldly to your friend to tell the truth. Remember, you can't control her response, but you can control your integrity and commitment to telling the truth. Your friend may need time, and that's okay. Remember that you are forgiven by God and that's what matters. Pray that He will heal your friend's heart and restore your friendship!

Love, Alena

2

Trustworthiness

Soul Scripture

> "The LORD detests lying lips, but he delights in people who are trustworthy."
>
> Proverbs 12:22

Snapshot

What is a food that you cannot stand—it grosses you out just by smelling it or seeing it, let alone eating it? Sushi might come to mind, or maybe squash casserole, or maybe crickets—a favorite food in some areas of the world!

There's a word that God uses to describe when you have a very strong dislike or hatred for something: *detest*. To *detest* is far worse than to *dislike* a food. In this verse, circle what God detests: "The LORD detests lying lips, but he delights in people who are trustworthy" (Proverbs 12:22).

Why do you think God hates lying?

Lying hurts our relationships. If someone lies to you, you cannot rely or depend on that person. And if you lie to someone, that person will feel they can't rely or depend on you.

But when a friend is trustworthy, she is worthy of trust. You can rely on her and know that she is telling the truth.

What is a food you love? Pizza made from scratch has such a delightful smell and taste! *Delight* is the opposite of *detest*. It means to find great pleasure in or to please greatly.

In Proverbs 12:22, when God uses the word *delight*, He is telling us what He delights in and finds great pleasure in—far beyond the enjoyment we have in foods we love.

In Proverbs 12:22 above, circle the word that describes what God delights in. Then fill in the blank: God "delights in people who are

_____."

Flipside

The opposite of trustworthiness is deceitfulness. Deceitfulness is when someone tricks another person or is misleading. A deceitful person is not trustworthy. Can you think of someone in the Bible who was deceitful? What about in your life?

In Genesis 37, Joseph was living in Canaan with his family. One day his brothers tricked him. They were jealous of all the attention Joseph was getting, so they threw him in a cistern, which is a large tank in the ground. Sadly, the brothers were hoping to get rid of him forever. They also deceived their father, lying to him about what happened.

TRUE or FALSE?	Because Joseph's brothers lied and were deceitful, things turned out well for them.

Things became a big mess for Joseph's brothers, and they even ran out of food at one point! Meanwhile, Joseph was found and sold into slavery in Egypt. But the Lord was with Joseph. Pharaoh, the leader of Egypt, had heard good things about Joseph and trusted him.

Joseph was honored because of his trustworthiness and was promoted to a high leadership position in Egypt. He went from being a slave to being a leader because of his trustworthiness. People knew they could depend on Joseph.

The same can happen in your friendships. Being trustworthy will help your friendships grow closer and deeper.

Trustworthiness is an important part of good friendships.

Unwind Your Mind

Why do you think it would be hard to build a friendship with someone who is deceitful?

_____

_____

_____

_____

_____

In your friendships, are you a trustworthy person?

_____

_____

_____

_____

_____

What Do I Do?

"Some people want me to hang out with them, but I have seen how they lie, so it doesn't seem like I can trust them. What should I do?"

—Bella

Dear Bella,

We all want to belong and feel a part of a group. So it can be difficult to avoid certain people, since we want to be included.

But who we hang around is a big deal. People start to rub off on us, and we become like the people we're around. So if people are in the habit of lying, we can start to think that a little lie here and a little lie there is okay.

We start normalizing things God detests. God tells us not to lie because it hurts our hearts. Sin hurts us, others, and our relationships. If your friends are lying, soon they will probably be lying to you too. And you might also join in on it.

It can be hard to separate ourselves from friends, but if they're lying and that's not the person you want to be, it's better not to spend time with them.

We are all sinful and fall short sometimes, so if a friend lies and comes clean about it, telling you they are sorry and want to be honest, that is different. We all need grace, and we can spur each other on toward honesty and truth. But if they keep lying, it would be wise to spend some time apart.

Make friends with people who value telling the truth, since God values it.

Love, For Girls Like You

> "How can I show my friend that she can trust me?"
>
> —Braelyn

Dear Braelyn,

Hey, girl. A good friendship is built on trust. We all want our friends to trust us, and the best way to show your friend she can trust you is to live a life that says that!

Some questions to ask yourself would be, "Am I speaking kind words to my friends? Do I stay away from gossip or engage in it? When's the last time I served my friend?"

If you're unsure about the qualities of a good friend, check out how Jesus lived His life. In John 15:12, Jesus commands us to love others as He has loved us. Jesus did not engage in gossip; in fact, He loved all people. He served the outcasts and the lowly. He was kind with His words and also truthful. His actions honored God and others.

In your friendships, Jesus is the perfect example to look to as you learn how to be a good friend. When you treat your friend how Jesus treated others, you will show her that she can trust you.

Love, Camryn

3

Loyalty

Soul Scripture

"For the word of the LORD is right and true; he is faithful in all he does."

Psalm 33:4

Snapshot

When a friend is loyal, or faithful, you know she has your back and that she will be there for you. She shows you allegiance and support.

Who is someone in your life who is loyal? _____

God is also loyal. In the Bible, when God spoke to His followers, He always told them the truth and did what He said He would do. They knew they could rely on Him. When Moses didn't think he had the ability to go to evil Pharaoh to free the Israelites, God told Moses in Exodus 3:12, "I will be with you."

Moses knew that God was loyal. So when God told Moses He would be with him as he approached Pharaoh, what did Moses do?

a) He ran away.

b) He trusted God.

c) He took a nap instead of going to Pharaoh.

Could you imagine God going back on His word and not being there for Moses like He said He would? That's one of the amazing things about God—He is loyal and never goes back on the truths of His Word. He indeed was with Moses and helped him lead the Israelites to freedom.

Circle the three words in Psalm 33:4 that show God is loyal: "For the word of the LORD is right and true; he is faithful in all he does" (Psalm 33:4).

God's Word is right, true, and faithful. The verse says that God "is faithful in _____ He does." What a relief! Doesn't it feel great knowing that you can trust God all the time, in everything?

What does it mean to be a loyal friend?

a) You should be able to depend on each other.

b) You can never depend on each other.

c) You can depend on each other from time to time.

When you and your friend are loyal, you should be able to depend on each other. Neither of you will be perfect, but you do your best to be there for each other in good and bad times, so *a* would be the correct answer.

Flipside

The opposite of loyalty is disloyalty or unfaithfulness. Someone who is disloyal or unfaithful turns their back on you, breaks your trust, and is not there for you.

An example of someone like that in the Bible is Judas Iscariot. In Matthew 26:14-16, we learn that Judas watched for opportunities to betray Jesus and to turn Him in. One day, Judas actually did hand Jesus over to the chief priests for money.

How do you think things ended up for Judas after being disloyal?

a) Everyone trusted him.

b) He had great friendships.

c) Things turned out terribly.

Matthew 27:3-5 says,

> When Judas, who had betrayed him, saw that Jesus was condemned, he was seized with remorse and returned the thirty pieces of silver to the chief priests and the elders. "I have sinned," he said, "for I have betrayed innocent blood." "What is that to us?" they replied. "That's your responsibility." So Judas threw the money into the temple and left.

The money Judas got from being disloyal meant nothing to him once he experienced the loss and pain of what he had done. He didn't even keep the money. Judas's disloyalty and the guilt he felt destroyed his soul and heart.

When someone is disloyal, that person can't grow deep friendships because there is no loyalty or trustworthiness to build on.

But Jesus had a lot of followers who were loyal and faithful in following Him. They were there for Him, stood up for Him, and supported Him. True friends are loyal and supportive.

Loyalty is an important part of good friendships.

Unwind Your Mind

Has someone turned their back on you and not been there for you? What happened?

When is a time you were a loyal friend, and when was a friend loyal to you?

What Do I Do?

> "For no reason, my friends stopped talking to our friend Carmen, and they want me to stop talking to her too. What should I do?"
>
> —Kanisha

Dear Kanisha,

I'm sorry you're going through this, Kanisha. This happens a lot in the elementary and middle school years. Friendships jump around a whole lot. Sadly, girls can be mean and exclude people for no reason at all.

The first thing you could do is think about how Jesus would feel about it. Ask yourself, "Would Jesus exclude Carmen and give her the silent treatment?" Since His second commandment is to love others, we can answer *no*, especially since Carmen did nothing wrong.

The second thing you could do is imagine if the roles were reversed and your friends stopped talking to you and tried to get Carmen to ignore you. How would you feel?

In Matthew 7:12, Jesus said, "So in everything, do to others what you would have them do to you." So Jesus is saying to treat others how you want to be treated.

And, if your friends are treating Carmen that way, they might also treat you the same way down the road.

If you are loyal to Carmen, she will probably be loyal to you and see the love of God in you. Other people will be drawn to being friends with you over time as they see that you are a loyal friend.

Know that God is with you as you work through this. He will guide you and lead you as you ask Him to. Hugs!

Love, For Girls Like You

"What should I do if my friend is being bullied?"

—Hazel

Dear Hazel,

Bullying is the worst, and I'm so sorry that your friend is experiencing that. It's common to not know what to do in this situation, especially if you feel afraid or unsafe.

First, I'd encourage you to tell a trusted adult, especially if you believe your friend might be in danger. To make someone aware of the situation can be the best thing to do a lot of times. Proverbs 31:8-9 tells us to speak up for those who cannot speak for themselves. If your friend is being bullied, she needs your support, encouragement, and possibly even your voice.

Pray and ask God to show you the best ways to support your friend. Maybe it's kind Scripture notes that remind her of the truth of who she is. Maybe it's speaking up, despite what others may think about you. It might just look like hanging out and providing a safe space for your friend to cry or process. If you're unsure, you can even ask your friend what she needs. The situation may be awful, but do not stress. God will provide you and your friend with all that you need.

Love, Kaitlyn

Supportiveness

Soul Scripture

"Rejoice with those who rejoice;
mourn with those who mourn."

Romans 12:15

Snapshot

Is there something you've really wanted but couldn't have? That can be difficult! In Luke 1, Elizabeth, Mary's cousin, knew that feeling too. She was very sad because she couldn't have a baby since she was old. But one day an angel appeared to Elizabeth's husband and told him she would have a baby!

After Elizabeth had been pregnant for six months, God sent the angel Gabriel to Nazareth to tell Mary that she would have a baby too—Jesus!

When Elizabeth and Mary learned of each other's great news, how do you think they responded?

a) They only cared about their own good news.

b) They celebrated with each other.

c) They competed with each other about who would have the best baby.

If you chose *b*, you're right! Instead of competing with each other, they were supportive of one another and celebrated together.

After Elizabeth had her baby, her neighbors and relatives shared in her joy. And when Mary gave birth to our Savior, Jesus, the angels broke out in celebration! The shepherds and all the people who heard the good news did too!

Romans 12:15 tells us to "_____ with those who rejoice" and to "_____ with those who mourn."

When a friend is mourning, or sad, it doesn't feel good if people around her are rejoicing. But she will feel comforted if friends are sad with her. In the same way, if a friend is celebrating, she will feel supported if her friends rejoice with her.

A friend is supportive when she notices her friend's feelings and shares them.

Flipside

Human instinct can make us feel jealous, or envious, of a friend. That is the opposite of being supportive. Instead of being excited for our friend, or being sad with her, we compare ourselves to her.

James 3:16 tells us, "For where you have envy and selfish ambition, there you find disorder and every evil practice."

What does James 3:16 tell us envy and selfish ambition lead to?

_____ and every _____ practice.

Feeling jealous stems from selfishness and wanting everything to be about us. It can be normal to feel this way, but it's important to change our mindset through prayer, memorizing Scripture, and choosing to be happy for our friends.

<table>
<tr><td>TRUE or
FALSE?</td><td>If your friend got a part in a play you wanted, it's supportive to be angry at her, give her the cold shoulder, and not talk to her.</td></tr>
</table>

You might feel like you want to ignore your friend if she got something you wanted. But Jesus calls us to be different from how the world tells us to be...Instead of being jealous, we should celebrate with our friends.

Which one of the following is a way you could choose to celebrate your friend, even if you feel jealous?

a) Bake your friend cookies to congratulate her.

b) Ignore your friend because you're upset.

c) Talk behind your friend's back about how she didn't deserve the part.

You might not feel like being happy for your friend, but when you choose to celebrate her instead of giving in to jealousy, your heart will naturally start to feel happier, And it will become easier to be a supportive friend. So, *a* would be the best answer.

Then, when it's your turn to be celebrated, your friend will probably be right there cheering you on too!

Supportiveness is an important part of good friendships.

Unwind Your Mind

? Is there a friend you are jealous of? How could you be supportive instead?

? When is a time you supported a friend by being sad with her or celebrating with her, or when is a time a friend supported you in this way?

What Do I Do?

"What should I do if I am jealous of a friend?"
—Alexandra

Dear Alexandra,

That is such a normal way to feel! Everyone feels jealous of a friend at one time or another. When a friend achieves something, scores higher than us, makes the team, has more friends than us, or something else, it can be easy to feel jealous.

One thing that can help is making a choice to celebrate with her and to be happy for her. Tell your friend congratulations, and treat her how you would want to be treated. Your heart will start to follow.

God tells us in His Word not to be envious or jealous because He knows we'll experience this feeling sometimes. We all do. But, as we fill our hearts and minds with God's Word about loving others, we will not compare ourselves to what our friends have as much. It will become easier to be selfless and celebrate with them.

And, the next time you have an achievement, your friends will be more likely to celebrate with you too!

Love, For Girls Like You

> "What if a friend leaves me out? I was best friends with a few girls, and now they don't talk much to me."
>
> —Emery

Dear Emery,

Whew, I hear you, friend. Being left out can feel awful, and I'm so sorry you're experiencing this. You opened your heart to people, and they didn't take care of it. It may feel like this defines who you are. Maybe you've started questioning if it's something you did or if it has something to do with how you look. Maybe you've even considered changing who you are so that they will come back. But you must know that this has nothing to do with your identity. Sometimes girls are just plain mean. Sadly, there's nothing we can do about that. Something you can do is ask God who *He* says you are. Let His truth wash over you. It's okay to cry with Him or even be upset. Be honest about how being left out makes you feel. He can hold all of it and fill the holes you may feel inside. As you find your footing again, begin to pray and ask God to send you friends who will love you the right way. Make sure to ask Him to prepare you for how to love those friends when He sends them. Much love to you, girl!

Love, Olivia

5

Peace

Soul Scripture

"A heart at peace gives life to the body."
Proverbs 14:30

Snapshot

Isn't it great to have peace in our relationships? When something is off or we've had an argument, it's unsettling. But when we feel good in our friendships, it creates a sense of calmness and peace.

When someone has godly peace, she trusts the Lord and has confidence in Him. A peaceful heart is one that is calm, not quick to get into arguments, and not easily angered.

Proverbs 14:30 says, "A heart at _____ gives _____ to the body."

Having a heart at peace brings life, joy, and honor to the Lord.

Do you know someone who finds a reason to get into an argument every time you're around them? Or someone who is always complaining about a situation? It can be tough to be around that kind of person! Let's think of an example, like a school party that was not planned well.

Circle the letter next to the sentence that is true for you:

a) I think a girl who complains about every little detail of the party and says how she could have done a better job would be fun to be around.

b) I'd want to hang out with a girl who makes the best of the situation even if things don't go her way and who enjoys the people she's with.

c) It would be fun to be with a girl who talks meanly about the party planners behind their backs and gossips about them.

Which kind of girl do you want to hang out with? Which girl are you most like? Which girl do you *want* to be like? Ask God to help you be a girl who is at peace and content. That attitude honors the Lord, and people usually want to be around people who are peaceful.

Flipside

Conflict is the opposite of peace. One of the things that starts arguments and conflict is not getting what we want. It happens when we want someone to agree with us but they don't, things don't go as planned, or we're just in a bad mood, so we start an argument.

Conflict can also happen when someone annoys or offends us, and we strike back instead of holding our tongue and being quiet. Sometimes it is good to speak up. But if you're just doing it to cause an argument, staying quiet is better.

Proverbs 17:14 says, "Starting a quarrel is like breaching a dam; so drop the matter before a dispute breaks out."

A dam is a structure that holds water back so flooding doesn't happen. So if you start a quarrel or argument, that's like opening a dam and letting the waters rush through. A dispute or fight is sure to happen.

What does this verse say to do to avoid starting an argument? It says to "_____ the matter before a _____ breaks out."

Circle all the options below that are ways you can drop the matter before an argument starts.

a) When someone makes you mad, retaliate and yell at them.

b) When someone makes you mad, take a breath and think before you speak.

c) When someone aggravates and annoys you, respond calmly.

d) Every time you are annoyed, make sure the person knows.

e) Don't let every comment bother you; like rain rolls off an umbrella, let the words roll off your back.

f) When you feel an argument brewing, ask God to help you be calm and at peace.

Remember that peace gives life to the body. So go out of your way to create peace in your friendships and not conflict. Options *b, c, e,* and *f* are ways that will help you do this. You and your friends will be much happier, and your friends will want to be around you more.

Peace is an important part of good friendships.

Unwind Your Mind

? Are you quick to rush into conflict? If so, how?

_____

_____

_____

_____

_____

? What are some ways you can have peace in your friendships?

_____

_____

_____

_____

_____

What Do I Do?

"When I'm in a group that is gossiping, what do I do?"

—Tamra

Dear Tamra,

It can be difficult when our friends talk about someone and we want to join in the gossip. But gossip can be like poison. It spreads subtly, but it hurts everyone in the end.

Something that can be helpful is to imagine the person standing there with you—how would she feel? If you would not share the same thing with her to her face, then it's best to not join in the conversation.

You can also ask yourself, "How would I feel if they were talking about me?" If it would bother you, then here are two things you can do:

1. You can walk away.

2. You can say something like, "Hey, guys, I don't want to talk about our friend while she's not here. I think that would hurt her." Then bring up another topic.

While friends might be annoyed, they'll probably realize they can trust you and might even admire you for trying to keep peace in the friendships.

Love, For Girls Like You

"How can I obtain peace in my relationships but still stand up for what is right?"

—Lila

Dear Lila,

This is such a good question! I want to tell you something that may shock you: Having peace doesn't necessarily mean that nothing is wrong.

Recognizing that something is wrong and standing up for what is right is how you make peace. The Bible calls us to be peacemakers (James 3:18). Staying silent in the face of evil doesn't keep peace at all; it actually destroys it.

When we chase after God and speak against evil, we make space for peace to enter into our friendships. Being a peacemaker isn't easy.

It can even be scary sometimes. But the peace you seek is found in righteousness—making things right.

Also, God grants us peace as we follow Him. If you have God in your heart, then you have unlimited access to peace! Spend time with God and ask Him to guide you. As you get to know Him, listen to His voice and His gentle nudging inside of you. Follow Him, and you'll make peace.

Love, Camryn

6

Patience

Soul Scripture

"Whoever is patient has great understanding, but one who is quick-tempered displays folly."

Proverbs 14:29

Snapshot

You know those times when things don't go your way—when your sibling is getting on your last nerve, your family is going through a tough time, you have loads of homework and don't understand any of it, no one will listen to you, or your friend is annoying you?

Those times are difficult, and it would be natural to respond with anger. But, in God's kingdom, we are taught another way—a better way. To have patience means you don't respond in anger but respond with a kind tone. You might feel angry, but you talk to that person about it, or you talk to God about it instead of letting the angry feelings explode.

If we respond to our friends in anger, how would they probably feel?

a) They would feel hurt.

b) They would feel frustrated.

c) They would feel loved.

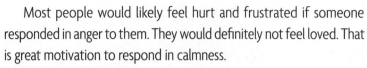

Most people would likely feel hurt and frustrated if someone responded in anger to them. They would definitely not feel loved. That is great motivation to respond in calmness.

In Proverbs 14:29, God says that "whoever is _____ has great understanding."

When someone is patient in life and in their friendships, they are wise and spread calmness, rather than chaos.

Jesus showed patience to His disciples when they didn't understand what He was teaching and when they doubted. Instead of reacting in anger, He explained things and kept walking by their side.

If your friend is annoying you, what is a way you could display patience?

a) You could scream and pull on your hair in frustration.

b) You could get angry at her and stomp off.

c) You could show patience by not saying anything, or by talking calmly with her about what's bothering you.

You might want to ditch your friend if she annoys you, but being a patient friend means you don't stop being friends with her when she annoys you, and you try to not respond in anger. Instead, you try to respond calmly by not saying anything, or you respond by talking with her about what's bothering you.

Flipside

Proverbs 14:29 tells us what the opposite of patience is: "One who is _____ displays folly."

Being quick-tempered is the opposite of patience. It means to react quickly with anger.

In Luke 13:14-15, the Pharisees were actually mad that Jesus healed a crippled woman on the Sabbath day, which was a day of rest:

> Indignant because Jesus had healed on the Sabbath, the synagogue leader said to the people, "There are six days for work. So come and be healed on those days, not on the Sabbath." The Lord answered him, "You hypocrites! Doesn't each of you on the Sabbath untie your ox or donkey from the stall and lead it out to give it water?"

The Pharisees responded without thinking and let their pride and frustration take over. But Jesus led with love and truth by healing the woman. Love was more important than anything to Him.

If we respond without thinking in our friendships because of being frustrated and quick-tempered, it hurts our friends.

It's okay to feel mad and angry—that is a normal feeling. But it's how we respond when we're angry that is important.

When your friend frustrates or angers you, what can help you be patient? Walking to the other room or talking to God can definitely help. God is so patient with us, and as soon as we ask Him for help, He will calm our hearts and help us respond calmly.

Patience is an important part of good friendships.

Unwind Your Mind

What are your trigger buttons—what causes you to be impatient and quick-tempered?

_____

_____

_____

_____

_____

What are some practical things that can help you be patient?

_____

_____

_____

_____

_____

What Do I Do?

> "When my friend is pushy, it makes me really frustrated and I can get pretty mad at her. What can I do to help?"
>
> —Bell

Dear Bell,

It can be really frustrating when friends (or siblings!) push our buttons. It's normal to feel agitated when your friend is pushy. But if we act on our frustrations by reacting in anger, we can hurt our friends' hearts and our own.

Here are some ideas of what you can do to avoid an argument and react with patience. See what works for you.

1. Take a deep breath to calm yourself.

2. Count to five to give yourself space to think twice about what to say.

3. Whisper a prayer to the Lord.

4. Say a Bible verse in your head.

It would also be helpful to let her know how her pushiness affects you. Check out the chapter on respect to find helpful steps on how to communicate this with your friend.

Patience is a fruit of the Spirit, so God will give you patience as you seek Him and ask Him for it. Becoming more patient will bring more peace to your life and friendships.

Love, For Girls Like You

"How do I even make a friend?"
—Mary Anne

Dear Mary Anne,

Listen, I'll be the first to tell you: Making friends can be hard! As an introvert (someone who enjoys their alone time), finding the right friends has been a challenge. I struggle to put myself out there out of fear of being awkward and stumbling through my sentences. I can just feel my palms getting sweaty now as I talk about it!

Despite my social awkwardness, God has provided me with just the right friends in the right seasons. He usually blesses me with more extroverted friends since they introduce themselves first. Sometimes, however, I have to be the one to introduce myself first. My encouragement to you: Do it scared! Walk up to the new girl and introduce yourself. Invite someone you're curious about getting to know over to your lunch table.

I know that making friends can feel scary or just annoying. (Like, why does it take so long?!) Creating strong and godly friendships takes time. You don't get to know anyone overnight! But in time, as you walk boldly, you'll find meaningful people to spend your time with.

Be bold and confident because God is with you. Any friend He wants you to make you will make! Remember, we don't need hundreds of best friends to have a full life. One or two or three close people is just fine.

Love, Alena

Kindness

Soul Scripture

"Love is patient, love is kind."
1 Corinthians 13:4

Snapshot

Kindness means being helpful, respectful, and considerate. Do you remember a time someone went out of their way to be kind to you? Kindness is memorable. There's a reason God defined love in 1 Corinthians 13:4 by saying, "Love is kind."

When we are patient with our friends, we choose to hold back—we don't react in anger. When we are kind, we act—we *do* something that uplifts a friend and makes her feel loved.

To show a friend kindness, it is helpful to know how she feels loved. One friend might feel loved when you say an encouraging, kind word. Another friend might feel loved when you bring her favorite gum to her or get her homework assignment for her if she is sick. Or a friend might feel cared about just by hanging out.

Rate these kind gestures from 1 to 5 based on how you feel most loved. Use 5 as the most and 1 as the least important way others help you feel loved. Next, ask a few friends to assign their own ratings. Write down the responses so you remember what acts of kindness mean the most to them.

Spending time together	1	2	3	4	5
Receiving a gift	1	2	3	4	5
Getting a hug	1	2	3	4	5
Encouragement	1	2	3	4	5
Someone helping you	1	2	3	4	5

Flipside

The opposite of kindness is meanness. While kindness means going out of your way to be kind and considerate, meanness means going out of your way to be mean.

While mean words and actions can come easily to us and people might think it's funny, we can quickly crush someone's spirit with a mean word.

Have you had someone tease you about something you can't do? That's what happened to Hannah in the Bible.

In 1 Samuel 1:6-10, Hannah wanted to be a mother but had a difficult time getting pregnant, so she was very sad. A woman named Peninnah teased Hannah year after year about not being able to have children.

In the middle of Hannah's sadness, Peninnah was mean-spirited and made Hannah feel even worse. Hannah would cry and pray to the Lord about it. The Lord ended up blessing Hannah with a child, but Peninnah made that season more difficult for Hannah.

What are two things a kind friend could have done for Hannah instead of what Peninnah did?

a) A kind friend could have reminded her that the Lord sees and loves her.

b) A kind friend could have kept laughing at Hannah.

c) A kind friend could have encouraged Hannah, reminding her that God would take care of her.

A kind friend would remind Hannah that God would always see her, love her, and provide for her. When someone chooses to be kind, that person reflects one of the fruits of the Spirit, kindness.

Kindness is an important part of good friendships.

Unwind Your Mind

Has someone been mean to you? Or was there a time you were mean to someone? What happened?

_____

_____

_____

_____

_____

What is a kind act someone did for you that made you feel loved?

_____

_____

_____

_____

_____

What Do I Do?

"How can I be kind to someone even when all my friends are being mean to them?"

—Andrea

Dear Andrea,

That's a good question! Girls sure can be mean sometimes. You are in a tough situation—you want to be included, but you don't want to be mean to a friend.

You might have heard the question, "What would Jesus do?" That is a great question to ask when you are unsure of what to do.

Jesus wasn't concerned about what people thought of Him. He only cared about what God thought, so He included people who were left out.

If people were being mean to you, how would that feel? What if one of your friends was kind to you despite what their friends were doing?

You could be kind to your friend by inviting her to sit with you at lunch or talking with her when others ignore her. God will take care of you and bless you for your kindness.

It could help to write Ephesians 5:1-2 on your bathroom mirror with a dry erase marker: "Follow God's example, therefore, as dearly loved children and walk in the way of love, just as Christ loved us and gave himself up for us."

Walk in the way of love like Jesus. We're rooting you on, sister!

Love, For Girls Like You

"How do I be kind to my friends even when they aren't being the nicest to me?"

—Eliza

Dear Eliza,

Whew, this is hard! God tells us in His Word to treat others the way we would like to be treated (Matthew 7:12). But just because God tells us to do something doesn't mean it'll be easy or that we'll even want to.

A part of being a godly friend means doing hard things, like treating our friends with kindness no matter what. Don't get me wrong, it is okay to acknowledge how someone's actions are making you feel. When friends are unkind, it hurts. It's our job to show others the love of Jesus despite that. We can't do it on our own, but with God's help and obeying His Scripture, we can make a difference in someone's life that they'll never forget.

Do you know what your friend will remember from this time in her life? Hopefully she'll recall how you loved her even though she was flat-out mean! And who knows how your kindness will impact her in years to come. It's not easy, but with God's help, you can love your friend well. Be the glimpse of Jesus she may not get to see otherwise.

Love, Kaitlyn

Gentleness

Soul Scripture

"Let your gentleness be evident
to all. The Lord is near."

Philippians 4:5

Snapshot

You know when a pleasant aroma fills the air, like hot cocoa, a lavender candle, or cookies in the oven? It can make you feel good, calm, and relaxed.

In the same way, when someone has gentle words, it calms the room and the soul. When someone is gentle, they speak with love in their hearts and have a tone that is considerate of the other person.

The Lord tells us in Philippians 4:5 to let our "gentleness be evident to _____."

To be a loving friend is to be gentle in how we speak and act toward our friends. Imagine that a friend accidentally spilled her drink on your favorite sweater. What would you do?

Which of the following is an example of a gentle reaction?

a) Yell at her, "What were you thinking! You're so careless!"

b) Calmly react by saying, "That's okay! We'll clean it up. It happens."

c) Throw your sweater in the trash and yell, "That was my favorite sweater! Get out of here!"

Option *b* would definitely be the better way to respond. When things don't go our way, it can be easy to overreact. But remember that the Lord is near and He can help you respond in gentleness.

Some friends are easier to speak gently to than others. But as this verse says, "The Lord is near." So that is great motivation to be gentle with those around you. He is with you and can help you.

Flipside

The opposite of gentleness is harshness. It's when someone acts rough and is unpleasant to be around. Have you ever had a cruel or harsh teacher, or been around someone like that? It affects the entire room. Instead of the pleasant smell of candles, cookies, or hot cocoa, the odor of rotten milk lingers in the air. Gross!

In 1 Kings 12:1-15, King Rehoboam of Israel chose not to listen to the wisdom of the elders regarding how he ruled, and he was harsh instead. His harsh response led to the division of Israel. Often a person's actions affect more than just themselves.

Just as harshness can break up a kingdom, a harsh or rough response to a friend can also break up a friendship.

Proverbs 15:1 says, "A gentle answer turns away wrath, but a harsh word stirs up anger."

Wrath is intense anger. What does this verse say turns away wrath? "A _____ answer."

And what stirs up anger? "A _____ word."

Harshness leads to conflict, drama, and division. But gentleness helps us have close, connected friendships and calms a situation.

Gentleness is an important part of good friendships.

Unwind Your Mind

? When is a time someone was harsh with you?

_____

_____

_____

_____

_____

_____

? When is a time you reacted with gentleness instead of harshness? How did it affect the situation?

_____

_____

_____

_____

_____

_____

What Do I Do?

> "What are practical and simple ways to show
> gentleness in everyday life?"
>
> —Camryn

Dear Camryn,

Great question! We can get so comfortable with how we respond that we don't even realize we're using a harsh tone with people we care about.

That's one of the reasons it's so important to read God's Word and to pray consistently. To treat our friends and family with kindness and gentleness, we have to work on it.

As we seek the Lord, our hearts will become more sensitive to how God wants us to treat our friends. The Lord will convict our hearts when we're being rude and need to speak with gentleness.

And the more we practice being gentle—having a kind tone and speaking the truth with love—the easier it will get.

You won't be perfect, but you will get better at it over time. Memorizing a Bible verse about gentleness will help you also. The Lord will bring it to mind right when you need it.

You could put Philippians 4:5 on a note card and tape it on your mirror. Then practice the verse as you brush your teeth. You'll be surprised how quickly you will memorize it and how it can help you speak with more gentleness.

And give yourself grace because it's a process—you got this!

Love, For Girls Like You

"Where in the Bible does it talk about having gentleness?"

—Meghana

Dear Meghana,

The Bible talks about gentleness more than 20 times. My favorite verse about gentleness is Matthew 11:29. Why? Because it reminds us that God is gentle. "Take my yoke upon you and learn from me, for I am gentle and humble in heart, and you will find rest for your souls." These are the words of Jesus.

God doesn't just call us to gentleness and leave us to figure it out. No! He lived it out first. Everything that God calls us to be, He *is*. How cool is that?

When God calls us to be gentle friends, we can look to Him as an example. A gentle friend is humble and puts others first. A gentle friend speaks with kind words that are sweet like honey and speaks the truth with grace. If you want to know what gentleness looks like, look at the life of Jesus. He was the best friend and serves as the best example for us in our own friendships.

Love, Camryn

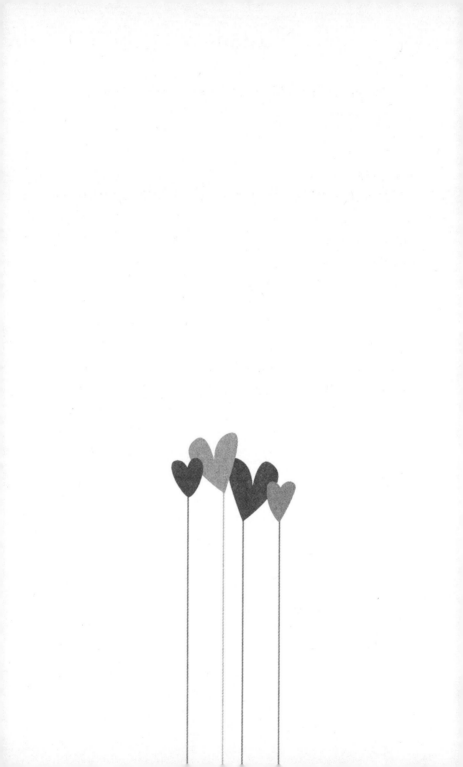

9

Self-Control

Soul Scripture

"But the fruit of the Spirit is love, joy,
peace, patience, kindness, goodness,
faithfulness, gentleness, self-control."
Galatians 5:22-23 ESV

Snapshot

Self-control is the ability to control yourself, especially when you don't get what you want.

Years ago, we couldn't order things online and receive them the next day or a few days later. We would have to wait a long time. Nowadays, we can usually have things our way, right away, which can make it more difficult to have patience and self-control.

Also, if you wanted to talk to a friend, there was usually only one house phone. So if your brother was on the phone when a friend called, your friend would get a busy signal and couldn't get through. Imagine the arguments that created between siblings!

But one of the benefits of that time was all the opportunities to practice self-control.

Galatians 5:22-23 shares qualities we can have when we know the

Lord. Circle the quality we're learning about today: "But the fruit of the Spirit is love, joy, peace, patience, kindness, goodness, faithfulness, gentleness, self-control."

Jesus practiced a whole lot of self-control when Satan tempted Him in the desert after being led there by the Spirit. Jesus had not eaten or had anything to drink for 40 whole days! Can you imagine that?

Every time Satan tempted Jesus to let go of self-control, Jesus used the Word of God to strengthen Himself and resist. Scripture is powerful! Let's use Scripture to help us like Jesus did. If you're tempted to let go of self-control and to gossip, look up Proverbs 18:8. It's a helpful verse to know.

Gossip hurts the person doing it and the person receiving it. If your friends are talking meanly about someone, what would it look like to have self-control?

a) Add to the gossip, making the person look bad.

b) Say that you don't want to talk about the person, or simply walk away.

c) Join in with the laughing.

Two options that would be much better than *a* or *c* above would be telling your friends that you don't want to talk about the person, or simply walking away. The other options would hurt your friend.

Reading and taking Scripture to heart is a great way to help us learn to have self-control.

Flipside

The opposite of self-control is impulsiveness, which is not having control. It can lead to not being able to resist something, even bad things for you.

Proverbs 25:28 says, "Like a city whose walls are broken through is a person who lacks self-control."

So, a person who lacks _____ is "like a city whose walls are _____ through."

A long time ago, walls would surround cities as boundaries to protect them. But if the walls were broken through, the city was no longer protected and could be attacked. In the same way, if someone has no self-control, there is nothing in place to protect the person.

When we are being pushy and need things now, it hurts us. But self-control is like a wall that protects our minds and hearts.

In the book of Esther, we learn about a woman named Esther, also called Hadassah, who had self-control. She was queen of Persia. There was also an evil, impulsive man named Haman who wanted to get rid of all the Jewish people.

Esther needed to talk to the king about Haman to stop the plan. But it was important for her to do it at the right time or the king wouldn't listen. She asked her community to pray for her, and she waited. After meeting with the king three times, she found the right time to bring up Haman's evil plan.

The king listened, and Haman was punished. After depending on prayer and having self-control to wait for the right time, Esther was rewarded.

Just as Esther had self-control, good friendships encourage self-control and doing the right thing.

Self-control is an important part of good friendships.

Unwind Your Mind

? Is there a time when you were pushy and didn't have much self-control? What happened?

_____

_____

_____

_____

_____

_____

? Is there a time you wanted to gossip or share something when the time wasn't right—but you had self-control instead? Write about it.

_____

_____

_____

_____

_____

_____

What Do I Do?

> "When I want to talk bad about someone to my friend, how can I have more self-control?"
> —Callie

Dear Callie,

There's a difference between venting with a close friend and gossiping, which is sharing stories that will spread to make someone look bad.

Is your intention to get something off your mind that is bothering you, or is it to spread a story or rumor about someone?

Usually gossip also includes sharing things that aren't true. But sometimes it can simply be sharing something bad about someone. You could be the person who chooses not to gossip and stops rumors from spreading.

Proverbs 18:8 is a good verse to remember in this situation: "The words of a gossip are like choice morsels; they go down to the inmost parts." Gossiping affects the heart deeply and hurts everyone involved. When someone gossips, they're not exercising self-control.

Callie, when you're wondering if something is gossip and you're thinking of sharing it, ask yourself these questions: "Would I still share it if the person was sitting here? And how would I feel if the person was sharing that about me?"

Ask God for wisdom too! He'll lead you.

Love, For Girls Like You

> "How can I control my words and actions
> when I'm upset with my friend?"
>
> —Anniah

Dear Anniah,

This is a great question! Controlling our words and actions seems to be the hardest when we are upset. Passion mixed with pain can be a recipe for a word disaster. I'll be the first to admit, self-control does not come easy. God knew this would be the case, though, so He filled the Bible with tools and instructions to help us live life filled with self-control.

The book of Proverbs compares life without self-control to a city broken into and left without walls (Proverbs 25:28). When we lack self-control, we leave an open door for chaos and pain. That's why when we are in the heat of an argument and lack self-control, we end up hurting people we love. Something you didn't even mean may have come flying out of your mouth, and before you knew it, you had hurt someone you never meant to hurt. When we lack self-control, our mouths are usually the first to tell us about it.

So how do we help ourselves? We have to retrain our reflexes and learn to control our responses. This requires time spent with God and in His Word. We get to ask God to help us, and as we spend time with Him, He will begin to rub off on us. The best way to become like Him is to spend time with Him.

Love, Olivia

Forgiveness

Soul Scripture

"Bear with each other and forgive one another if any of you has a griev-ance against someone. Forgive as the Lord forgave you."

Colossians 3:13

Snapshot

Circle the four-letter word in the word *forgive*. Do you see it?

The word is *give*. Forgiveness is something *given* to someone when they don't necessarily deserve it.

There are two aspects of forgiveness that are important in friendships:

1. forgiving others

2. asking for forgiveness

It can be hard to forgive a friend when she hurts you, but a rela-tionship can't exist without forgiveness. Since we are all imperfect, at some point we will be the ones who hurt our friends too, even if we don't mean to.

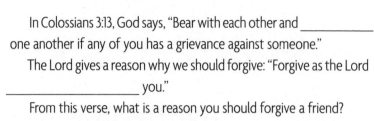

In Colossians 3:13, God says, "Bear with each other and _____ one another if any of you has a grievance against someone."

The Lord gives a reason why we should forgive: "Forgive as the Lord _____ you."

From this verse, what is a reason you should forgive a friend?

a) You should work it out so you can still have pizza together Friday night.

b) You should forgive your friend because she gave you a really cool gift.

c) You should forgive because you have also been forgiven through Jesus.

We can forgive because we have also been forgiven through Jesus. And when we have hurt others, it's important to ask our friends if they will forgive us.

Once we have worked through a conflict with them, we might want to keep bringing up how we were hurt, but it's important to move on and move forward. The wisdom in Proverbs 17:9 tells us, "Whoever would foster love covers over an offense, but whoever repeats the matter separates close friends."

So, what is the result of bringing up a matter, or disagreement, again and again?

a) It makes you closer to your friend.

b) It separates close friends.

Bringing up something again and again after it has already been worked out is like a constant dripping on a rainy day—it's annoying, and it can create separation between you and your friend. Once you have forgiven one another, let love cover over the offense, or mistake, and move forward.

Flipside

The flipside of forgiveness is unforgiveness, which means not allowing any errors and not forgiving someone.

Unforgiveness hurts our hearts and friendships.

In Matthew 18:23-35, Jesus tells a story about a man who owed his master ten thousand bags of gold but couldn't pay him back. The man begged the master to forgive the debt his family owed. The master felt bad for the family, so he forgave their debt.

After the forgiven man left, he saw that a servant owed him 100 silver coins. What do you think the man who had been forgiven did?

TRUE or FALSE?	The man overflowed with kindness and forgave the servant, just as he had been forgiven.

No! The man actually did not forgive the servant's debt. Can you believe that? Don't you want to tell him, "The master just forgave you! You should also forgive the servant!"

Instead, the man threw the servant into jail. The man quickly forgot about the forgiveness that had been shown to him.

Remember the master who had shown the man forgiveness? Well, he heard about this man's unforgiveness and actually threw him into jail! What is the point of the story?

a) Forgive just as you have been forgiven.

b) Do not forgive someone—ever!

c) When the master comes, run away from him.

Option *a* is the correct answer because, just as we have been forgiven, God wants us to forgive.

Forgiveness is an important part of good friendships.

Unwind Your Mind

Is there someone you haven't forgiven? Write to God about it.

_____

_____

_____

_____

_____

Who is someone who has forgiven you? How did that affect your friendship?

_____

_____

_____

_____

_____

What Do I Do?

"A girl at school keeps being mean to me and hurting me. Do I just keep forgiving her?"

—Lauren

Dear Lauren,

That's a really good question. I am sorry you're experiencing that—that is really hard! If your friend keeps on being mean to you and doesn't try to change, then that is not a good friendship. And she is not someone you should keep trying to be friends with.

You can forgive her, but it's okay to not be friends with her. It's important to have boundaries around your heart to protect it when someone doesn't take care of it.

When a friend who has been mean asks you for forgiveness, it doesn't mean they won't hurt you again, but it is a sign that they are making efforts to treat you right. Forgiveness is an essential ingredient for close friendships because each of us will mess up at times. But if your friend keeps hurting you, you might need space and distance from that person. You can have time away from that person and still have forgiven them.

If you have bitterness and anger toward her and gossip about her, then that is not a sign of forgiveness, and that will only tangle up your heart. If you feel that way, talk to God about it and a trusted person in your life. They can help you.

When you forgive, it doesn't always have to be said to the other person. If the situation is not a healthy, safe one, then it is okay to just forgive the person in your heart. But it can be helpful to talk to the person if you are able to.

Forgiveness will free your heart.

Love, For Girls Like You

"How can I forgive someone even when they really hurt me and I'm not sure I will ever forget it?"

—Christina

Dear Christina,

Hey, friend. Being hurt by someone can be incredibly painful. Yet it's inevitable.

No matter how hard we try not to be, we will experience heartbreak in friendship. Maybe your friend said some cutting words to you, or her actions betrayed you. It can be hard, but God has called us to forgiveness. Not only that, He has forgiven us. You and me. Let's look at Colossians 3:13 again. It tells us to forgive each other just as God has forgiven us. Remembering that we, too, have sinned and hurt others helps us put ourselves in our friend's place. How would it feel if God decided not to forgive you?

Don't get me wrong. Forgiveness does not mean allowing your friend to continue to hurt you. Forgiveness does mean, however, not holding your friend's mistake over her head. Chances are, your friend feels incredibly sorry. Choose to forgive and pursue peace. Not only for the sake of your friend but for you too! Unforgiveness causes bitterness to take root. Choosing to forgive preserves your heart and might just be the light your friend needs.

Love, Alena

Respect

Soul Scripture

"Do to others as you would
have them do to you."
Luke 6:31

Snapshot

When a friend has respect for others, she treats them in a way that shows she cares about their feelings and well-being. In good, healthy friendships, friends respect and consider one another's feelings.

It can be hard in a friendship when we don't get our way and a friend doesn't do what we want them to. But if we are pushy and try to make a friend do something, give the silent treatment, or make them feel guilty to get our way, we are not respecting them or being considerate of them.

Good friends give others freedom to make their own choices without trying to make them feel bad or guilty for their choices.

For example, if you really want a friend to come over to your house but she says she is too tired to get together, there are a few different ways you could respond.

A way to show respect would be to:

a) Text or call your friend repeatedly until she agrees to hang out.

b) Tell her that if she was a good friend she would come over anyway.

c) Tell her that you understand and hope she gets some rest.

How would you want your friend to treat you if you were too tired to get together? In Luke 6:31, Jesus said, "Do to others as you would have them do to you." These words of wisdom are also called the Golden Rule. It is a great verse to help us show respect to our friends. When we respect each other's boundaries, we are loving one another.

Flipside

While respect means to consider a friend's feelings, disrespect means to not consider someone's feelings.

Have you heard of a woman named Abigail in 1 Samuel 25? She stopped a massive fight from happening. She was married to a rich man named Nabal. David had been a shepherd and protected Nabal's land and sheep. When David needed help with food and supplies, he asked Nabal, but Nabal refused to help David and his men.

David gathered his men and was preparing to fight Nabal. Meanwhile, Abigail respected how David had protected them, so she quickly gathered bread, raisins, fig cakes, and other supplies to bring to the men.

David appreciated and respected Abigail for what she did, so he decided not to attack. He said, "Praise be to the LORD, the God of Israel, who has sent you today to meet me. May you be blessed for your good judgment" (1 Samuel 25:32-33).

What good judgment did Abigail show?

a) She brought raisins to the men instead of broccoli.

b) She showed respect for David and his men by bringing them supplies.

c) She joined Nabal in his selfishness and only looked out for herself.

Abigail showed good judgment by respecting David and giving him the help he needed. Showing respect can lead to peace in our friendships, while disrespect can lead to chaos, hurt, and division.

Respect is an important part of good friendships.

Unwind Your Mind

When is a time someone disrespected you? What happened?

_____

_____

_____

_____

_____

When is a time someone respected your boundaries? How did it help your friendship?

_____

_____

_____

_____

_____

What Do I Do?

"How do I tell my friends I feel disrespected when they make fun of me all the time?"
—Shauna

Dear Shauna,

I'm sorry you're going through that. That is really hard when friends make jokes at your expense.

Communicating with your friends about your boundaries and what hurts you will help your friendships be healthier and stronger.

This can be uncomfortable to do, but communicating your feelings will become easier over time, and it is helpful for your friends to hear the truth about how their actions affect you.

Sometimes friends don't know that they have hurt us until we tell them. Talking face-to-face is a lot better than over text so things said aren't misunderstood.

When you talk to your friend, it can help to:

1. First let your friend know something you appreciate about her, because it can be hard to hear something negative about ourselves.

2. Tell your friend how it affects you when she makes fun of you.

3. Share that her friendship matters to you and that is why you're sharing this with her.

If things don't change and she keeps making fun of you, it's important to keep your boundaries and to find friends who don't do that.

You should feel good, respected, and cared about in your friendships when you're together and when you're apart.

We're rooting you on, Shauna!

Love, For Girls Like You

"What if people make fun of me for believing in Jesus?"

—Isabella

Dear Isabella,

As Christians, we're not promised respect from others. In fact, the Bible warns us of the persecution we will experience when we honor God as our King. John 15:19-20 tells us the world hates those who are not of the world. When we decide to live like Jesus, that may rub people the wrong way. Those who hate God will hate us. It doesn't feel good to be hated, but God promises to give us His strength. One day, when we enter eternity, there will be no more persecution. Only love. And love is what we are called to here on earth.

Next time you are being made fun of, return the insults with the love of God. Rather than fighting back, pray. Pray that they will come to know the love of God, and ask God how to show it to them. This won't be easy, but God's power is made perfect in our weakness. Through Him, we have the strength to make it through persecution and love others despite it. Try to find one or two friends who believe in Jesus, too, and encourage each other. We were made for community, and God can use our friendships to encourage us.

Love, Camryn

12

Generosity

Soul Scripture

"Each of you should give what you have decided in your heart to give, not reluctantly or under compulsion, for God loves a cheerful giver."

2 Corinthians 9:7

Snapshot

When someone acts with generosity, they are being kind and freely sharing what they have without expecting something in return. They go above and beyond what is expected.

It says in 2 Corinthians 9:7, "Each of you should give what you have decided in your _____ to give, not _____ or under compulsion, for God loves a _____ giver."

Have you had a friend who shared something with you reluctantly, or hesitantly, not really wanting to? That's not a good feeling. But if someone is cheerful and excited to give, they aren't forced to give—they want to give. That feels a whole lot better.

TRUE or FALSE?	God wants you to be a sad giver and tightfisted with your things.

God wants us to be cheerful givers! God also says not to give under compulsion—feeling like you have to give—but out of love.

In Mark 12:41-44, Jesus told us about a widow who gave out of love. Jesus sat down by the temple treasury watching people give their money. While many rich people gave large amounts, a poor widow gave only a few cents, but it was all she had.

> Calling his disciples to him, Jesus said, "Truly I tell you, this poor widow has put more into the treasury than all the others. They all gave out of their wealth; but she, out of her poverty, put in everything—all she had to live on" (Mark 12:43-44).

It wasn't the amount she gave that mattered to God but that she gave from her heart. Money isn't the only thing we can give generously. We can also give of our time, talents, words, and in other ways.

Flipside

The opposite of generosity is stinginess, which means being ungenerous and holding on tightly to our things. We should be wise in our giving but not tightfisted with our things.

Everything we have is a gift from God. He didn't intend for us to be tightfisted, unwilling to share.

Proverbs 23:6-7 (HCSB) says, "Don't eat a stingy person's bread, and don't desire his choice food, for it's like someone calculating inwardly. 'Eat and drink,' he says to you, but his heart is not with you."

This proverb is saying, "Don't eat a _____ person's bread" because that person is more concerned for the things he's giving away than he is concerned for the person who might need what he has. He doesn't really want to share.

The problem is that "his _____ is not with you."

Do you see a theme here? Jesus was pleased with the widow because she gave out of love, willing to and wanting to share. The stingy person's heart was not with his guests. Generosity helps us love others well.

Generosity is an important part of good friendships.

Unwind Your Mind

When is a time you were stingy? How did it make you feel?

_____

_____

_____

_____

_____

_____

Is there a time you were generous to a friend or she was generous to you? Share about it.

_____

_____

_____

_____

_____

_____

What Do I Do?

"How can I be generous with my time and resources without feeling burnt out?"
—Sarah

Dear Sarah,

Sometimes we can give so much of our time and talents that we feel burnt out just like you said. You might have felt that way? God doesn't want that. If we feel burnt out and tired from giving, then we are no longer giving out of love but out of fumes.

As you seek the Lord and ask Him for wisdom on how to give, He will show you. It's okay to say no to people sometimes if you need time to regroup and energize. When we're running on fumes because we are doing too much, then we'll have a harder time loving the Lord and loving others.

We get to be cheerful givers. To do that, we need to have energy and balance in our lives. Spend time with the Lord, and He'll show you the way.

Love, For Girls Like You

"How can I make sure I'm being generous from the right part of my heart?"

—Juliana

Dear Juliana,

Ooh, girl! This is a great question.

Making sure the motives of our heart are right is important to God. Matthew 6:1 warns us to be careful not to do the right things because we want to be seen. If we do, we will have no reward from God in heaven. God makes it clear that just because we do the "right" thing doesn't mean we're doing the right thing. Our generosity should come from a place of compassion and kindness. If our desire to be generous is actually self-seeking (if we make it about us), then our generosity means nothing!

A good way to check if your motives are pure is to ask yourself: "Am I doing this for God or for myself?" If your answer is "myself," don't be ashamed. Simply ask God to help change your heart. Everything we do should stem from our love for Him! As you fall more in love with Him, your heart will start to look more like His.

Love, Kaitlyn

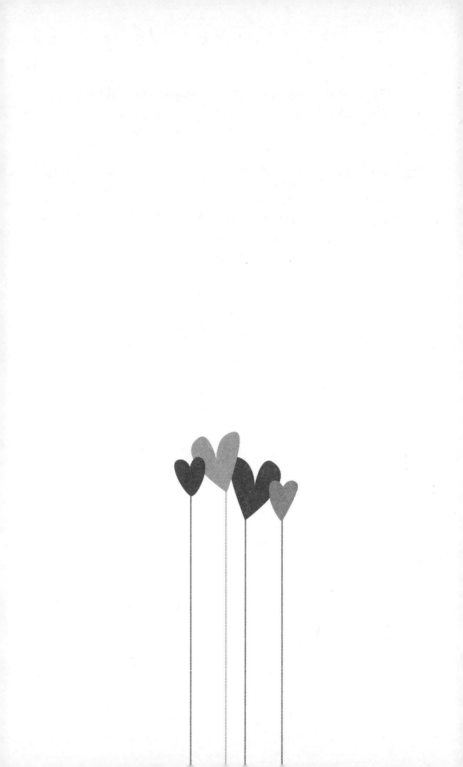

Encouragement

Soul Scripture

"Therefore encourage one another
and build each other up."
1 Thessalonians 5:11

Snapshot

One of the sweetest ways we can love our friends is by encouraging them, which means to give them support or hope. It helps our friends feel loved and confident.

In 2 Timothy 1:3-7, Paul, a follower of Jesus, encouraged Timothy to use his spiritual gifts and to keep on walking strong in his faith. This is a great way to encourage a friend in their faith.

Circle all the ways below that you could encourage your friend.

a) Give her a Scripture that will lift her up.

b) Tell her nice things that aren't true just to make her feel good about herself.

c) Bake her cookies.

d) Share with your friend what you love about her.

e) Gossip and talk behind her back.

f) Show her you care by spending time with her.

Some great ways to encourage your friend are *a, c, d,* and *f.* First Thessalonians 5:11 says: "Therefore _____ one another and _____ each other up."

The word *therefore* means there is a reason we can encourage our friends. Let's look at the reason that is found in the verse before: "He died for us so that...we may live together with him" (1 Thessalonians 5:10).

That is why we can encourage one another—Jesus gave His life for us so we can be with Him forever. So no matter what we are going through, we can always have hope in the Lord and encourage others!

Flipside

Proverbs 16:24 tells us that "gracious words are a honeycomb, sweet to the soul and healing to the bones." Let's come up with the opposite of the verse. What do you think it would say?

"_____ words are _____,

_____ to the soul and _____ to the bones."

One idea is "<u>Discouraging</u> words are <u>poison, painful</u> to the soul and <u>hurtful</u> to the bones."

Discouraging and critical words can roll off our lips in two seconds, but hurt a person's spirit for a long time. Discouragement steps on someone's spirit and can cause them to lose their confidence.

The Lord doesn't want us to do that. If we have a chance to build up our friends or tear them down, let's build them up! You can encourage your friend's heart and soul just by loving like the Lord and sharing His words with her.

In Judges 4 and 5, the Israelites had forgotten about God and were being treated harshly by the leader Sisera. The Israelites were discouraged and cried out to the Lord, so He raised up a woman named

Deborah to help them. She was a prophetess and relayed God's messages to the people.

She told a man named Barak that God was calling him to lead the army against the evil Sisera. Barak felt discouraged and was too afraid to go, so he asked her to come with him.

In Judges 4:14, Deborah encouraged Barak to walk in God's ways by saying, "Go! This is the day the LORD has given Sisera into your hands. Has not the LORD gone ahead of you?"

Friends who encourage us to walk strong in our faith like Deborah are great friends to have.

Encouragement is an important part of good friendships.

Unwind Your Mind

How has someone discouraged you in the past?

_____

_____

_____

_____

_____

What are ways you can encourage your friends? What are some ways someone has encouraged you?

_____

_____

_____

_____

_____

What Do I Do?

> "My friends speak meanly to me and don't encourage me. What do I do?"
>
> —Shamika

Dear Shamika,

I'm so sorry your friends are treating you that way. That's really painful. Friendships can be hard!

Good friends should encourage us with their words or actions. While they won't be perfect, they spend a lot more time being kind and encouraging to us than being mean.

You can talk to your friends about how they are treating you, and see if it changes. If it doesn't, it's time to find new friends. You deserve better.

Good friends know your worth and value. Spend time with friends like that. You are a child of God, and you should be treated that way. It might take a little time to find friends like this, but it's worth the wait.

Pray about having encouraging, godly friends and watch what God does!

Love, For Girls Like You

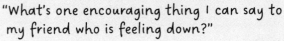

"What's one encouraging thing I can say to
my friend who is feeling down?"

—Stella

Dear Stella,

There are plenty of encouraging things to say to our friends who are down. Knowing just the right thing to say can feel like a lot of pressure. The truth is, any encouragement is good for the soul. Another version of Proverbs 16:24 (NLT) says, "Kind words are like honey—sweet to the soul and healthy for the body." If your friend is down, *any* kind word may be just the thing to lift her up. Consider complimenting a character trait of hers. Maybe you love the way she treats people or adore how intentional she is. You could leave a note card in her locker that says something like "You are loved." Sometimes we just need to be reminded that someone sees us and loves us. It may not completely change her mood, but you can trust that God will use your honey-like words to uplift her soul.

Love, For Girls Like You

14

Vulnerability

Soul Scripture

"'My grace is sufficient for you, for my power is made perfect in weakness.' Therefore I will boast all the more gladly about my weaknesses, so that Christ's power may rest on me. That is why, for Christ's sake, I delight in weaknesses, in insults, in hardships, in persecutions, in difficulties. For when I am weak, then I am strong."

2 Corinthians 12:9-10

Snapshot

Vulnerability is risking being open and showing emotion despite being afraid.

Wanting to be liked can make us hide away from being honest about who we are. But if we do that, we won't be able to build true, deep friendships.

In 2 Corinthians 12:9, God says, "My grace is sufficient for you, for my power is made perfect in_____." For this reason, the apostle Paul said he chose to "boast all the more gladly about my weaknesses, so that Christ's _____ may rest on me...For when I am weak, then I am _____."

God's kingdom can seem upside down and backward sometimes, like when the Scripture says, "When I am weak, then I am strong." But that is just saying that when we lack things, Christ's power can fill those holes.

Part of being vulnerable is sharing our struggles and joys with a friend. It could mean sharing with a friend how you feel hurt by her. It can take practice to be open like this, but it can help to make your friendship stronger.

If your friend hurts you, what is a helpful way to respond?

a) You should yell at her.

b) Give her the silent treatment and never share what's wrong.

c) Talk to her and share your feelings.

Talking with your friend about your feelings can be helpful. On a scale of 1 to 5 (with 5 being the highest), how do you do with sharing your feelings when a friend has hurt you? _____

Many times when friends hurt us, they don't even know it. They can't read minds, so if we don't share it, they might never know. We don't need to share every little thing that bothers us, because sometimes we just need to let things roll off our shoulders. But if your friend has really hurt you, it can help to be honest and vulnerable.

Being open and honest with our friends about our emotions can create closer and stronger friendships.

Flipside

The flipside of being vulnerable is being guarded, or closed off. Protecting our hearts from wrong things is smart. But if we feel safe with a friend and stay guarded, then we won't have deep friendships.

Sometimes people think that in order to be liked they need to appear perfect. Actually, the opposite is true. When we are honest about our shortcomings and struggles, people can feel more connected to us because they struggle too.

TRUE or FALSE? **To make good friends, we need to appear perfect.**

TRUE or FALSE? **To make real friends, we can open up about our struggles.**

To make true friends, we can open up about our struggles. Do you remember Judas, who we talked about earlier? He was deceptive and not open about his struggles. He even sat at dinner with Jesus and the other disciples while hiding his greed and sinful desires to turn Jesus in for money.

After turning Jesus in, Judas ended up feeling remorse and regret, but it was too late to protect Jesus. Judas could have trusted Jesus and been open with Him, but he was closed off and it hurt him.

When you find safe friends to share your heart with, vulnerability will help you and your friends grow closer.

Being vulnerable is an important part of good friendships.

Unwind Your Mind

? Are you closed off and guarded with your friends? Why?

_____

_____

_____

_____

_____

? Is there a friend you want to open up to about something? Write about it.

_____

_____

_____

_____

_____

What Do I Do?

> "How do I know if it's safe to be vulnerable with a friend?"
>
> —Grace

Dear Grace,

Great question! It's important to know if a friend is safe to be vulnerable with and open up to. Sometimes we won't know until we step out in faith and try being open. You can start out sharing smaller things and seeing if you can trust her with that. Does she make fun of you? Is she distracted and not listening to you? Does she go and tell other people something you asked her not to? These would all be reasons to not be vulnerable with that person.

But if your friend listens to you, doesn't tell people what you shared (unless they need to tell an adult because it is hurtful to you), and doesn't make fun of you but has compassion, then you could probably be vulnerable with her.

Being vulnerable can be hard at first, but it will get easier over time. You will find joy in growing deeper and closer friendships.

Love, For Girls Like You

"How is vulnerability good for me?"

—Alison

Dear Alison,

This question challenged me! If I'm being honest, vulnerability is not a natural strength of mine. Being open with someone about my feelings is just plain scary! *But* being open about our emotions is so good for us. I can't deny that. God created us to live in community with others, and true community involves true vulnerability. What is friendship without honesty and trust? Just a soundboard of meaningless noise! When we are honest and open in our friendships, we are able to grow. Friends who are vulnerable with each other are able to experience growth, healing, and meaningful encouragement. If no one ever knows what I'm going through, how am I supposed to get through it?

We need people. We need help. In order for someone to check on us, pray for us, or even love us, they have to know who we really are, what we're really going through, and what we really need. I'm not saying it's easy to be vulnerable. Trust me, I know. I am saying, however, that vulnerability is absolutely worth it. It's good for you, friend. Rely on Jesus to give you the boldness to let someone else in. If you're not sure who to be vulnerable with, begin to pray that God will show you the friends you can trust.

Love, Alena

15

Humility

Soul Scripture

"Sitting down, Jesus called the Twelve and said, 'Anyone who wants to be first must be the very last, and the servant of all.'"

Mark 9:35

Snapshot

Human nature is to only think of me, me, me. What do *I* want and what will make *me* happy? But people who have humility consider others, too, and are not just wrapped up in themselves.

Being humble also means being dependent on God and knowing you need Him. They recognize that God is all powerful and they aren't.

Jesus knew the disciples were concerned about themselves and who was the best, so in Mark 9:35, He said, "Anyone who wants to be _____ must be the very _____, and the servant of all."

Jesus wanted the disciples to stop trying to be first in everything. He wanted them to be humble.

Circle examples of a girl showing humility.

a) *She only wants to play her game, thinking she has the best ideas and won't listen to others.*

b) *She knows other people have good ideas too, so she is open and listens.*

c) *She is dependent on God and gives Him the glory for her achievements.*

d) *She thinks she is the best and doesn't need God.*

e) *She wins a game against her friends and tells them over and over that she is so much better than them.*

f) *She wins a game against friends and doesn't brag but tells them, "Good game!"*

Options *b*, *c*, and *f* are great ways to show humility. The Lord will help you reflect humility a step at a time when you ask Him to.

Flipside

The opposite of humility is pride, which means thinking you are better than others and don't need to depend on God. Proverbs 11:2 says, "When pride comes, then comes disgrace, but with humility comes wisdom."

So, with humility comes _____.

But with pride comes_____.

Disgrace means having shame and people thinking poorly of you. In Luke 18, Jesus was around a group of people called the Pharisees who were prideful and confident in their own righteousness, so He told them a parable, or story:

Two men went to the temple to pray. One of them was a Pharisee. He stood up and thanked God that he was not like the sinners around him and shared about the righteous things he had done.

Well, Jesus didn't like that very much. The Pharisee was actually saying how much better he was than others...in a prayer to God!

The other man, the tax collector, knew he was a sinner. In humility, he pleaded, "God, have mercy on me, a sinner" (Luke 18:13).

Which of the following do you think Jesus was pleased with?

a) Jesus was pleased with the tax collector's humility.

b) Jesus was pleased with the Pharisee's pride.

> Jesus said, "I tell you that [the tax collector], rather than the [Pharisee], went home justified before God. For all those who exalt themselves will be humbled, and those who humble themselves will be exalted" (Luke 18:14).

Wow! So those who humble themselves, God will lift up, yet those who have pride will fall. We can apply this wisdom in our friendships. No one wants to be around someone who thinks they're better than everyone else and looks down on others.

In humility, be considerate of your friends' needs and wants, and your friendships will grow. Knowing that you need God and are dependent on Him will also keep you humble.

Humility is an important part of good friendships.

Unwind Your Mind

? Why do you think it can be difficult to be around prideful people?

_____

_____

_____

_____

_____

? Why is humility a good quality to have?

_____

_____

_____

_____

What Do I Do?

"How can I be humble when I feel really proud of something I've done?"

—Jenny

Dear Jenny,

Excellent question! There's a difference between being confident and being prideful. Confidence is a good thing. When you have worked really hard and achieved something, it's awesome to celebrate. Enjoy it!

Miriam celebrated with her brothers, Moses and Aaron, after they crossed the Red Sea and were freed from the Egyptians. They didn't praise themselves, but they celebrated and praised the Lord with singing and dancing.

Yes, part of your achievement is from your hard work, but a huge part of it is from God giving you breath and strength to be able to accomplish it. So, remember to thank the Lord and give Him glory and praise when you accomplish great things.

When pride creeps in, we can start feeling like our achievement is only because of what we did and that we are better than other people—a feeling of superiority. That's what Jesus was saying not to do.

It benefits us to have a humble reliance on the Lord and to not look down on others. So, yes, celebrate your accomplishments, Jenny, and enjoy them! Just remember to praise the Lord for them too!

Love, For Girls Like You

"How can I stay humble even when I feel like no one is noticing my achievements?"

—Kat

Dear Kat,

Great question, my friend. If we're being honest, we all want to be noticed. We all know that feeling we get when someone we admire compliments us. It gives us that pep-in-our-step glowing feeling! It's natural to want someone to call out the good in you. It's natural to desire to be seen. This is probably why the Bible talks so much about humility!

Humility means to be selfless, thinking about others rather than ourselves. When we think about our image more than we think of others, our hearts become filled with pride. The Bible warns against this in Philippians 2:3. Jesus tells us to do nothing out of our own self-ishness. Instead, He calls us to live in humility—putting others before ourselves. When we live this way, we're able to see others and make a difference in the world! When you start to wonder if anyone is notic-ing your achievements, look to God. Remember that He sees you, and that's actually enough! Put your energy into loving someone else and thinking about them.

Love, Olivia

16

Flexibility

Soul Scripture

> "Trust in the LORD with all your heart and lean not on your own understanding; in all your ways submit to him, and he will make your paths straight."
>
> Proverbs 3:5-6

Snapshot

Flexibility is an awesome quality to have in friendships. It means to adjust easily to change with a good attitude. When someone is stuck in their own way and can only see what they want, it can be annoying. Flexibility is something most people have to work on.

One thing that can help is to trust in the Lord and not lean just on what we think we should do. That can help us go with the flow more. Instead of being tightfisted, someone is openhanded and understands the Lord is leading them.

Proverbs 3:5-6 says to "trust in the _____ with _____ your heart and lean not on _____ own understanding; in all your ways submit to him, and he will make your paths straight."

As we lean on the Lord's wisdom and trust Him, we know God is leading us, so we can relax and enjoy the day more.

Let's say the plans you and your friends made for dinner change. Which girls' reactions are flexible?

a) "I'm not going to that restaurant. I don't like that one."

b) "Sure! That's not my favorite restaurant, but I'm up for trying it again."

c) "We can meet at a restaurant, or at your house or mine to hang out. I'm good with whatever."

d) "I just like being at home, so I'll only meet there."

e) "I'm doomed! This day will be awful now."

f) Think to yourself, "That's not what I wanted to do, but the Lord's leading me, so I'm going to make the best of it."

Options *b*, *c*, and *f* are examples of reactions that are flexible and would end up helping everyone enjoy themselves more!

Flipside

The flipside of flexibility is rigidity. When someone is rigid, they are set and fixed on their ways and don't change.

In the last chapter we talked about the Pharisees. They were rigid and set in their ways. Jesus kept trying to rid them of that. The Pharisees trusted in themselves, so there wasn't room for flexibility. But followers of Jesus trust in the Lord, so there is room for change as we depend on God to lead us.

In friendships, rigidity pushes people away because people who are rigid are really hard to be around. They tend to be selfish, while people who are flexible are generally easier and more fun to be around.

People who are rigid have a harder time growing in their faith because it can be difficult to trust the Lord in the unknown when things are not clear. But that's what faith is: trusting God even when we don't understand everything.

Let's look at some scenarios that are more difficult to be flexible in. Circle the reactions that show flexibility.

a) "My family is moving. I feel sad, but I'm going to trust the Lord is going ahead of me."

b) "Noooooooo!!! I'm not moving. I'm staying here. Not moving an inch."

c) "I'm soooo mad I have no friends in my classes. This will be the worst year of my life!"

d) "I'm not in any classes with my friends. I'm bummed about it, but Lord, help me be a light in this new class and make new friends."

As you can see, flexibility is appealing and makes friendships and faith easier and more enjoyable. Reactions *a* and *d* are flexible and open to the Lord's leading.

Flexibility is an important part of good friendships.

Unwind Your Mind

What is the problem with rigidity and not being flexible?

Are you a flexible person? How could you be more flexible with friends and in faith?

_____

_____

_____

_____

What Do I Do?

> "If you have known someone a long time, does that mean you have to be good friends?"
> —Amanda

Dear Amanda,

Good question, Amanda. Sometimes we can think we have to live by certain rules, like being good friends with someone just because we've known them for a long time. But we don't.

Things change over time, and we change too. As we change, we will grow apart from some friends, which is natural and okay. Even relationships in the Bible changed over time. It's a part of life.

We should still be friendly with that person and not ignore them. It's important to be a kind person who is not cliquey and only includes certain people.

But you don't have to be best friends with that person. If she is making ungodly choices, it is okay to create more space between you two and not hang out. If she's still nice but you don't feel as close to her, it's also okay to hang out with different people.

Be flexible, and see who the Lord brings to your path. Pray for the

Lord to guide your friendships and to show you who He wants you to be good friends with.

Love, For Girls Like You

"How do I handle a friend who is unwilling to compromise or make time for me?"
—Kendra

Dear Kendra,

This is a good question, and a common problem in friendship! It can be hurtful when you feel like you're giving your all in a friendship, but your friend isn't doing the same. You're not crazy for feeling this way. Godly friendships are built on love and care. And the truth is, you need someone to pour into you as much as you pour into others. If you feel that your friend isn't making time for you, I'd encourage you to kindly vocalize that to her. She probably has no idea that you're feeling this way, so be sure to ask questions and be honest about how you're feeling. Remember to put on love before and during your conversation (Colossians 3:14). If you're not the best with words, try writing out how you're feeling in a letter. Chances are, she'll understand and make an effort to spend time with you.

If your friend doesn't receive your honesty, that's okay. It may mean you don't spend as much time together, but continue to pray for her and love on her when you can. Find a few friends who make time for you and love you enough to compromise! They're good for your soul, and we all need those kinds of friends.

Love, Camryn

Compassion

Soul Scripture

"Therefore, as God's chosen people, holy and dearly loved, clothe yourselves with compassion, kindness, humility, gentleness and patience."

Colossians 3:12

Snapshot

Colossians 3:12 shares some important qualities to have, knowing we are holy and dearly loved by God. The verse says to "_____ yourselves with _____, kindness, humility, gentleness and patience."

Did you recognize some of the qualities we have already learned about in this verse? Circle the ones we have already learned.

When someone has compassion, they are concerned about someone else's hurt or suffering. Have you heard of the story of the Good Samaritan? Jesus shared this parable to teach the importance of having compassion for others and loving your neighbor.

In Luke 10, a man was on his way to Jericho when he was attacked by robbers. Two people walked right past the man and didn't help him.

A third man, who was a Samaritan, felt bad for him and stopped and bandaged his wounds. He brought the man to an inn and took care of him. He also gave money to the innkeeper to take care of the hurt man.

In Luke 10:36-37, Jesus asked, "'Which of these three do you think was a neighbor to the man who fell into the hands of robbers?' The expert in the law replied, 'The one who had mercy on him.' Jesus told him, 'Go and do likewise.'"

When Jesus said to *go and do likewise*, He was saying:

a) Only think about yourself, and do not be concerned about others.

b) Wait and see what everyone else is doing.

c) Show compassion for someone who is hurt by helping them.

When our friends are hurting, it might be inconvenient to stop and help them if we don't want to miss out on what everyone else is doing, but good friends show compassion.

Flipside

If someone is not compassionate, they are indifferent and don't care. If a friend shows indifference, they might not pay attention to someone's hurts, or they might totally ignore them.

When a friend shares her hurt with you, if you are indifferent and don't listen, she will think you don't care. When you listen and respond, that is showing compassion, and you will be showing your friend that you love her.

Sometimes a friend gets left out on purpose or something happens where she can't participate. What are some ways you could show compassion to her?

a) Check on your friend and make sure she's okay.

b) Run off with your other friends and ignore your hurt friend.

c) Sit with your friend and show her you care.

Sitting with your friend or checking on your friend are two ways you could show compassion. Imagining being in your friend's situation is a great way to help you be compassionate and think of what your friend might need. When you show compassion to your friends, they will probably be compassionate to you as well.

Having compassion is an important part of good friendships.

Unwind Your Mind

Has there been a time when someone didn't care that you were upset? What was that like?

_____

_____

_____

_____

_____

How did it make a difference in your life when someone showed you compassion?

_____

_____

_____

_____

What Do I Do?

> "What do I do when my friend is upset or sad?"
>
> —Delah

Dear Delah,

This is a great question. It makes me think of Galatians 6:2: "Carry each other's burdens, and in this way you will fulfill the law of Christ."

When your friend is upset, you can help her carry that burden, that hard thing, by being there for her. One way you can do that is by listening. It might make her feel better just to vent about what's upsetting her.

Sharing encouraging words can help too, like saying, "I'll be praying for you," or "It will be okay," or sharing a Scripture with her. But everyone is different—some people like to hear encouragement when they're sad, while others just want you to listen. You can ask your friend how you can best support her—if she'd like encouragement or just wants you to listen.

Sending her an encouraging card or baking her cookies can also make her feel loved. Simple, compassionate gestures like these will remind your friend that she is cared about. And sometimes a friend just needs a hug. Sending hugs to you, too, Delah!

Love, For Girls Like You

> "How can I show compassion to a friend who's
> hurting when I don't know what to say?"
> —Tait

Dear Tait,

Showing compassion is essential to being a godly friend. You may be tempted to overthink what to say or how to say it when your friend is hurting. But you know what? When I was going through a hard time after my mom died, what mattered most to me was just that my friends were there. It's okay to not know what to say. By simply making yourself available and showing your friend that you're not going anywhere, you are showing compassion. Sometimes words are helpful, but they're not always necessary. Simple things like kind gestures, her favorite snack, or a note card with some encouragement can be meaningful to your friend. Above all, pray. Pray for your friend and whatever she is going through. God loves her more than you ever could, so voice your concerns to Him because He cares for her.

Love, Kaitlyn

18

Joy

Soul Scripture

"Rejoice in the Lord always.
I will say it again: Rejoice!"
Philippians 4:4

Snapshot

When someone has joy, they have a deep feeling of pleasure and happiness. Philippians 4:4 tells us: "Rejoice in the _____ always." It's a lot easier to be happy when things are going well for us. But when things are harder, it can be really easy to be anything but joyful.

That's why the Lord shares a key word in Philippians 4:4. Circle which one finishes the verse. Rejoice in the Lord...

 a) ...when you're eating your favorite meal.

 b) ...when all is going well and you get just what you want.

 c) ...always.

When someone follows Jesus, joy comes from trusting in the Lord and finding contentment and happiness in Him.

Joy also comes from knowing that you are loved by God. It doesn't mean you won't feel sad. But it means when you have those times, you have a steadiness and peace that you are held in the arms of God, who loves you deeply.

Joy and laughter in friendships can lift up your spirits, right when you need it. Friendships can be a safe haven and refuge in the midst of difficulty.

Proverbs 17:22 says, "A cheerful heart is good medicine, but a crushed spirit dries up the bones."

So having a _____ heart is good _____.

When you're not feeling joyful, sharing with the Lord what you're grateful for can help shift your mindset to joy.

Flipside

The flipside of joy is misery—a feeling of great distress and discomfort. Misery can come when we're ungrateful, only focus on what's going wrong, or don't follow God. Just like a small spark can set a huge forest on fire, each of those things hurts our friendships.

Jonah is an example of a man in misery. God had wanted Jonah to preach to the sinful city of Nineveh. But Jonah didn't want to go, so he didn't listen to God and ended up in the belly of a huge fish! I can imagine that would be an awful place to be!

> From inside the fish Jonah prayed to the LORD his God. He said: "In my distress I called to the LORD, and he answered me. From deep in the realm of the dead I called for help, and you listened to my cry" (Jonah 2:1-2).

Jonah was then thrown out of the fish, and guess where he went? Yep, Nineveh. At first, God was going to destroy the city of Nineveh because of all the awful sin, but after Jonah preached about the Lord, they turned from their evil ways and repented, and God showed compassion on them.

Sadly, Jonah decided to stay in his misery and was mad that God had compassion on the people, even though God also had compassion on Jonah. That was not good for Jonah's friendships or heart.

When we trust the Lord in our friendships and walk in His ways, a deep joy will fill our hearts. Instead of being a friend filled with misery, which is hard to build a friendship on, be a friend filled with joy and gladness, and people will be drawn to you.

Joy is an important part of good friendships.

Unwind Your Mind

If you feel miserable, what is a way you can rejoice in the Lord?

_____

_____

_____

_____

_____

How can you bring joy into your friendships?

_____

_____

_____

_____

_____

What Do I Do?

"How can I have joy even when my friends are negative?"

—Hayden

Dear Hayden,

That is a great question, and it can be a challenge for sure! It can be hard to be joyful when our friends are negative. We can enjoy our friendships a lot more when we have joyful, grateful hearts. Do you see the root word of "enjoy"? JOY.

We talked earlier about how a small spark can set a large forest on fire. A negative word can do the same. It's also like a line of dominoes—it affects the next person and the next person and spreads to everyone. But joy can do the same thing!

So, Hayden, try to switch things around and set a tone of joy in your friendships. You can do this by looking at the bright side of things and not complaining, but having a spirit that chooses joy, no matter what happens.

When your friends see you rejoice in the Lord, it might just rub off on them! It would also help to find a friend who has a joyful spirit to encourage you too.

Love, For Girls Like You

> "How do I have joy even when I'm walking through something really sad?"
>
> —Kara

Dear Kara,

Hey, friend. Ugh. Walking through something sad is my least favorite thing to do! Truthfully, I sometimes wish life was just a long path of rainbows and tasty candy. We know, though, that in this life we will face hard things.

Whether you're going through a big thing or a little thing, life can be sad. But take heart! With God's Spirit in us, we are promised the gift of hope! And that hope produces joy. Joy is deeper than happiness, and it doesn't always look like a big grin plastered on our faces. The beautiful thing about joy is that it has nothing to do with our circumstances. The Bible tells us in Romans 15:13 that God fills us with joy, hope, and peace as we trust in Him. No matter what life is throwing at us, we have access to hope, which means we have access to joy. When you accept Christ into your heart, you can trust that this life here on earth is not the end. The sad things here are temporary. It doesn't mean they won't hurt or that you won't be sad, but it does mean that you have the hope of heaven with God. That's why you can have joy despite your circumstances.

Next time you feel hopeless, remind yourself that you have hope because you have God. Rejoice because you know that this life isn't the end!

Love, Alena

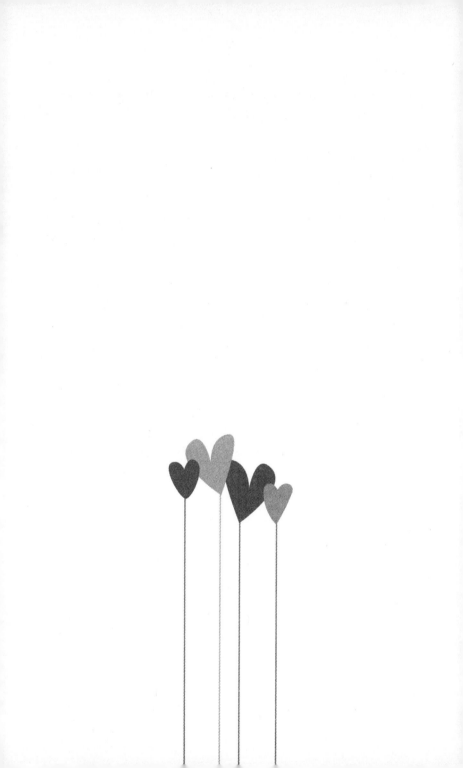

19

Like-Mindedness

Soul Scripture

"Finally, all of you, be like-minded, be sympathetic, love one another, be compassionate and humble."

1 Peter 3:8

Snapshot

When you and a friend are like-minded, you share similar goals, interests, and values. You also usually agree on what is right and wrong, which makes it easier to get along and grow in your faith together. We know that Jesus thought it was important to be around like-minded people because in Luke 10:1, He sent His followers out "two by two," which would help them feel strong and supported.

First Peter 3:8 says, "Finally, all of you, be _____, be sympathetic, love one another, be compassionate and humble."

In Acts 2:42, 44-47, the believers were like-minded. Let's look at some of the activities they did together. Circle each activity you see.

They devoted themselves to the apostles' teaching and to fellowship, to the breaking of bread and to prayer...All the believers were together and had everything in common. They sold property and possessions to give to anyone who had need. Every day they continued to meet together in the temple courts. They broke bread in their homes and ate together with glad and sincere hearts, praising God and enjoying the favor of all the people. And the Lord added to their number daily those who were being saved.

The believers were like-minded and grew in their faith together through fellowship, teachings, communion, giving, meeting together, eating together, having glad and sincere hearts, and praising God.

These were all things that helped them grow closer to each other and grow in their relationship with God. As you think about the girl you want to be, try to be around people who are like-minded who will help you grow in your faith.

Flipside

The flipside of being like-minded would be different-minded—having different values, goals, and ideas of what right and wrong are.

Put an *x* over the things that describe people who would be different-minded, and circle ones that would be good, like-minded friends to spend your time with. Someone who...

steals from others	is honest
makes fun of others	is considerate
wants to grow in her faith	makes fun of believing in God
gossips and spreads rumors about people	is compassionate when others are hurting
is critical and mean-hearted	is kind and encouraging

Can you start to see what like-minded friends would look like? It doesn't mean that you or your friend will make all good choices in life, but it means that you both are trying to make good, godly choices and grow in your faith. You can both encourage and spur one another toward this goal.

Like-mindedness is an important part of good friendships.

Unwind Your Mind

? What are some qualities you do not want in your friendships?

_____

_____

_____

_____

_____

_____

? What are good qualities that you see—or would like to see—in your friendships?

_____

_____

_____

_____

_____

_____

What Do I Do?

"How do I make godly friends with similar values?"

—Amy

Dear Amy,

It can be hard to not have godly friends. It's a big encouragement when a friend knows Jesus and can encourage your faith.

Here are some ideas on how to make godly friends:

1. Going to activities where there will be other believers puts you in places where it is easier to make godly friends. Going to church is a great place to start. You can also go to church activities, youth group, Bible study, service projects, or volunteer with your church.

2. When you're at school, sports practice, or another activity, notice others who seem similar to you. People usually are drawn to other people who are like-minded. If you notice a girl who is kind and encouraging, you'll probably want to spend time with her, and she might be a believer also!

3. If there are Christian clubs at your school, that can be another great way to meet other believers.

That's wonderful that you want to have godly friendships with people who have similar values. God will bless that!

Love, For Girls Like You

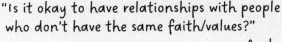

> "Is it okay to have relationships with people who don't have the same faith/values?"
> —Ansley

Dear Ansley,

Great job asking this question, girl! This can feel like one of the trickiest things to navigate in our friendships. Don't worry, the Bible has the answers for us! Scripture tells us that we are to be wise about our friendships. In 1 Corinthians 15:33 it says that "bad company corrupts good character," and 2 Corinthians 6:14 tells us not to be bound together with unbelievers because light and darkness can't fellowship. When we look at the life of Jesus, we see that He spent time with lots of unbelievers. Some even called Jesus a friend of tax collectors and sinners. As Christians we are called to lead others to God! Who are we leading, if not sinners? When you befriend those who don't believe in God, you should desire to lead them to Christ.

When we look at who Jesus's closest friends were, though, they were His disciples. Jesus spent significant time with them. Your closest friends, your best friends, should share your faith in God. They can help build you up and encourage you with the Word of God.

Love, Olivia

20

Goodness

Soul Scripture

"Let us not become weary in doing good, for at the proper time we will reap a harvest if we do not give up."

Galatians 6:9

Snapshot

Have you ever run a race? When you run a race, you usually get to a point where you hit a wall. You don't actually run into a wall, but you feel like you do because you get very tired and aren't sure if you can finish the race.

Galatians 6:9 encourages us, "Let us not become weary in doing _____, for at the proper time we will reap a _____ if we do _____ give up."

Goodness is making right, good choices. This verse tells us that we will reap a harvest if we continue doing good. That means that a whole lot of fruit and good things will come as a result. When our friendships are filled with goodness, our hearts and character will be more like the Lord.

Just like when we hit a wall while running, if we feel tired of pursuing goodness in our friendships, what actions below can help?

a) Being honest with a friend that we need some encouragement can help.

b) Just giving up and making bad choices can help.

c) Reading verses like Galatians 6:9 and asking God for help can uplift you.

Being honest with a friend and the Lord about needing help can restore you. Striving for goodness might feel tiring after a while, but if it's motivated by love, it's a lot easier. As Mother Teresa, a follower of Jesus, once said, "Wash the plate not because it is dirty or because you are told to wash it, but because you love the person who will use it next."

Doing the good, right thing is easier to keep doing when you are motivated by loving God and others. And it also helps when you have friends who are pursuing goodness and making good choices as well.

Flipside

The flipside of goodness is badness, which means doing the wrong thing.

You become like the people you hang around, so who you spend time with matters. First Corinthians 15:33 says, "Bad company corrupts good character." If you spend time with people who are doing the wrong thing and making bad choices, that can corrupt and influence your character.

The flipside of this verse is that good company encourages good character. So, if you make friendships with people who are pursuing good character, you will want to do that more too.

Proverbs 27:17 also tells us, "As iron sharpens iron, so one person sharpens another."

This verse is saying:

a) If we are around people with sharp fingernails, we will have sharp ones too.

b) If we need our pencils sharpened, our friends can sharpen them.

c) Being around people who are godly will help us be godly.

When we are around people who have goodness and make good, wise choices, we are more likely to do the same.

Goodness is an important part of good friendships.

Unwind Your Mind

Is there a time someone who made bad choices rubbed off on you? What happened?

_____

_____

_____

_____

_____

Which of your friends makes good choices? Why would it be good to spend time with her?

_____

_____

_____

_____

What Do I Do?

> "What do I do if my friends are making bad choices, but I don't want to look weird by doing the right thing?"
>
> —Rachel

Dear Rachel,

It feels good to be included, doesn't it? But being on the outside sure feels lonely. When our friends are making bad choices, it's natural to want to be liked by them. But if we have to make wrong choices to do that, that can really hurt us.

God wants us to care most about pleasing Him. Galatians 1:10 says, "Am I now trying to win the approval of human beings, or of God? Or am I trying to please people? If I were still trying to please people, I would not be a servant of Christ."

Pleasing the Lord matters more than having friends' approval. If we want to serve the Lord, then part of that is caring most about what the Lord thinks. Sometimes we will look weird to our friends and the world when we make good, godly choices, but that's okay.

It's okay to stand out when it's because we're following God. God will bless and honor that. In Acts 17, even though people were making fun of Paul for preaching the gospel, a woman named Damaris didn't follow the crowd, but chose to believe. She was a strong woman who cared most about the Lord.

Spend your time around people who are making good, godly choices, and you will do the same. Cheering you on, Rachel!

Love, For Girls Like You

> "How can I encourage my friends to make good choices without sounding judgmental?"
> —Blakely

Dear Blakely,

Hey, girl! Friendship should make us better people. It is your job to encourage your friends! We can't control how our friends will respond when we challenge them to make a different choice. We *can* control how we deliver the challenge to our friend. Our encouragement should first be saturated in love. First Corinthians 13:4-8 tells us what love is. Love is kind, patient, and filled with truth. When you feel the urge to encourage your friend to make a better decision, your words should be filled with kindness, patience, and truth. Approach your friend humbly and lead by example! Make sure your life aligns with what you're encouraging your friend to do. Be sure to encourage your friend in private and lead with love. Pray and ask God for wisdom and to guide your words. Friends make each other better, and I'm thankful for friends who challenge me!

Love, Kaitlyn

21

Gratitude

Soul Scripture

> "Give thanks in all circumstances; for this
> is God's will for you in Christ Jesus."
>
> 1 Thessalonians 5:18

Snapshot

Gratitude is being appreciative and thankful. Have you heard the saying "The grass is greener on the other side"? It means that we think another person has things better than we do—their "grass" looks greener and better than ours.

But, if we look, we can usually find green grass right where we are standing. It's a matter of looking and choosing to see what God has already given us.

If we aren't content and satisfied with what God has given us, we'll always be looking for the next best thing, the next best friend. But, if we have gratitude, we have peaceful hearts that are grateful for what God has given us.

First Thessalonians 5:18 says, "Give thanks in all circumstances; for this is God's will for you in Christ Jesus."

So what is God's will for us? "To give _____ in _____ circumstances."

He doesn't necessarily say to give thanks *for* all circumstances, but to give thanks *in* them. With the Lord, we can always find things to give thanks for. What can you have gratitude for right now?

A spirit of gratitude in our friendships will stop us from competing with our friends, too, and we'll be more satisfied with what God has given us.

> TRUE or FALSE? | If I have gratitude, I will be more focused on what I don't have.

When we are grateful, we don't have as much time to think about what we don't have because we are giving thanks for what God has given us.

Flipside

The flipside of gratitude is ingratitude. Someone who has ingratitude is ungrateful and tends to grumble and complain. They always expect more and don't appreciate when they do get things. They are difficult to satisfy. People who are ungrateful tend to be unhappy and might not have a whole lot of friends.

In Exodus 16 and 17, God had just set the Israelites free from 400 years of Egyptian captivity. They were on their way to the promised land. Instead of being grateful, Exodus 16:2-3 says that "in the desert the whole community grumbled against Moses and Aaron. The Israelites said to them, 'If only we had died by the LORD's hand in Egypt! There we sat around pots of meat and ate all the food we wanted.'"

The Israelites were in a difficult situation, but God still provided what they needed when they needed it. However, the Israelites could only see what they didn't have. The first thing they did was grumble, and the next thing they did was long for their old situation. They compared and kept looking at the past, and it made them ungrateful.

Looking back and longing for what was, or looking around and wanting something different, builds ungratefulness in our hearts. But talking to God when we are sad and then giving thanks for what we do have builds a grateful heart.

Which of these are examples of a grateful heart?

a) Enjoy your favorite food—and then ask for it every night after that.

b) Be grateful for a great dinner and then go with the flow with what you have the next night.

c) Even though you're not too excited about the meal, you choose to give thanks for what God has provided.

d) When you get to have dessert but don't get all the toppings you want, you complain.

e) When you get to have dessert (even without all the toppings you want), you give thanks.

f) You long for what your friends have, and you keep asking your parents about it.

g) While you may want what your friends have, you are happy for them and grateful for what you do have.

h) You get stuck in the place of wishing things were how they used to be.

i) You talk to God when you wish things were how they used to be, and you switch your mindset by giving God thanks.

Options *b*, *c*, *e*, *g*, and *i* are great examples of choosing gratefulness. When you choose to be grateful in imperfect situations, you may even be happier than if you had gotten your way, because gratefulness breeds contentment.

Unwind Your Mind

When is a time you were ungrateful? Did it lead to peace and contentment or frustration and unhappiness?

_____

_____

_____

_____

_____

_____

What are some ways you can practice being grateful?

_____

_____

_____

_____

_____

_____

What Do I Do?

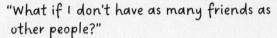

"What if I don't have as many friends as other people?"

—Lucy

Dear Lucy,

Seeing that some people have more friends than you can be hard. But it can be difficult to be close with so many people at once. While it might seem like someone has a ton of friends, many times, they're probably not that close with them all.

It is better to have a few close friends who know you and appreciate you than many friends who don't know you that well. Remember how when Jesus sent His disciples out to share the gospel, He sent them out in groups of two—not in large groups? There is something valuable about spending time with just a few friends.

When you start to feel ungrateful and compare, choose to give thanks for what God has given you instead.

You could write your friend a note about why you are thankful for her. Or bake her some cookies to let her know you appreciate her. These are simple ways to change your mindset from ungratefulness and what you don't have to gratefulness and what you do have.

Hugs, For Girls Like You

> "How can I have gratitude even when there's so much to complain about?"
>
> —Priscilla

Dear Priscilla,

Great question! Did you know that gratitude is a command in the Bible? We're told in 1 Thessalonians 5:18 to give thanks in all circumstances. This means that no matter what, there is something to be thankful for.

I get it. We live in a world that is constantly reminding us of all that is wrong. And if we're being honest, there is a lot wrong! Because of this, we tend to forget all of the things that are right in our world. We don't spend enough time thinking about what is good! And trust me, there is a lot of good. Don't fall for the lie that there is nothing to be grateful for. There are blessings all around us; we don't even have to look very hard. Seemingly small things like breath in our lungs or a body that works are actually very important things to be thankful for. Blessings like having a home or a family that loves us, food to eat, good friends, and an able body are a couple more.

It's true, life isn't perfect, but there is a lot to thank God for. If the Bible commands us to be thankful, it must be important and good for us. Have you ever tried being grateful when you're in a funky mood? Something as simple as listing off your blessings can help shift your mindset to praise. Our God is good, and His goodness is on display all around us!

Love, Camryn

22

Discernment

Soul Scripture

> "And this is my prayer: that your love may abound more and more in knowledge and depth of insight, so that you may be able to discern what is best and may be pure and blameless for the day of Christ."
>
> Philippians 1:9-10

Snapshot

Discernment means using good judgment to decide what is right and best. When someone has discernment, she understands what the right and wrong thing to do is in a situation.

In Philippians 1:9-10, the apostle Paul says, "And this is my prayer: that your _____ may abound more and more in knowledge and depth of insight, _____ that you may be able to _____ what is best and may be pure and blameless for the day of Christ."

When we are confident that we are loved by God, we can make better decisions. We don't need to impress others because we know God loves us.

In the list below, discern which kinds of friends are good ones to hang out with and then circle them. Someone who...

lies to her parents

acts mean to other kids but is nice when adults are around

pursues God and wants to grow in her faith

is honest and trustworthy

treats you poorly and criticizes you

values you by being kind to you

Flipside

The opposite of discernment is foolishness—not being able to discern what is best in a situation. If someone acts foolish, they are not using good judgment.

Proverbs 13:20 says, "Walk with the wise and become wise, for a companion of fools suffers harm." This proverb is saying that when you hang out with people who act foolish and are not discerning, you will suffer harm and become like them.

Who you hang around determines who you become. It's important to discern which friends are good to be around and which ones are harmful. Ask yourself these questions:

1. "Do my friends draw me away from God?"

2. "Do they pressure me to make wrong decisions?"

3. "Are they mean to me?"

If you answered *yes* to these questions, then they are not good friends. Ask God to provide you with friends who draw you closer to God, encourage you to do the right thing, and are kind to you.

This story reflects the importance of those you hang around:

Once there was a father who gave his son an old, antique watch. He told the boy to find out how much he could get for his special watch. The boy came home after bringing it to a thrift store and said, "Dad, they said they would only give me five dollars." The father told him to try a watch store. So the boy went to the watch store. When he came home, he was frustrated and said to his dad, "They said they would only give me five dollars too!" The dad then told the boy to try the museum. The boy ran home from the museum and yelled excitedly, "Dad, they said they would give me a million dollars for the watch!" The boy's dad told him that he had finally found a place that knew the watch's value.

In the same way, good friends know your value. Do your friends know your value and worth?

Discern which friends appreciate you and love you well, and spend your time with them. And spend time with the God of the universe who chose to create you, values you, and gave His Son's life for you so you could be with Him forever.

Discernment is an important part of good friendships.

Unwind Your Mind

When is a time you didn't use discernment but acted foolishly instead? What did you learn?

_____

_____

_____

_____

_____

_____

Who are some people in your life who value you? How do they make you feel valued?

_____

_____

_____

_____

What Do I Do?

"How do I know if someone wants to be my friend, and how do I discern if a friendship is healthy?"

—Kelly

Dear Kelly,

Awesome question! Discerning and knowing if someone wants to be your friend is important. Our friendships won't grow if we spend

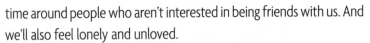

time around people who aren't interested in being friends with us. And we'll also feel lonely and unloved.

Building healthy friendships is like playing tennis. After hitting the ball over the net, you wait for the other person to hit the ball back— you're not the only one hitting the ball. In the same way, when you're building a good friendship, it takes both of you. Each of you should put effort into building the friendship.

You can ask yourself some questions:

1. "Am I the only one who tries to make plans to get together, or does my friend also?"

2. "Does my friend try to be around me at school, or am I usually the one who is looking for her?"

3. "Is she nice to me, or does she make fun of me?"

These questions will help you discern who wants to be friends and who doesn't. And, if someone doesn't want to be friends with you, that's okay! Because you are *so loved* by God. There are so many other girls who will want to be friends with you. Take time to invest in those people who see how wonderful you are.

You won't want to be close friends with every single person you meet, either, and that's okay! God made each of us unique, so we connect more with certain people.

And remember, it takes time, so don't rush it. When we rush our friendships, they might not last. But when you let a friendship build naturally at its own pace, then it will more likely develop into a good, healthy friendship over time.

You are loved!

For Girls Like You

"What do I do if a friend is trying to get me to do the wrong thing?"

—Zoe

Dear Zoe,

Whew, friend, this can be hard. When friends encourage us to sin, it can feel hard to say no. Sometimes our loyalty to a friend can get in the way of our obedience to God.

One simple question to ask yourself might be: "Do my friends encourage me to obey or disobey God?"

If the answer is disobey, you may want to reevaluate your friendships. If you love God and want to obey Him, the people you surround yourself with should encourage you to do that, not discourage you! Creating some distance may be necessary if you are always facing temptation from your friend. Look for godly friends who will encourage you to obey God.

When a friend is encouraging you to make a poor choice, that is a great opportunity to lead by example. Rather than listening to them, ask God to give you the strength to obey Him. Through your obedience you get to show your friend what it looks like to live a life of obedience to God.

Love, Kaitlyn

23

Selflessness

Scripture

> "Everyone should look out not only
> for his own interests, but also
> for the interests of others."
> Philippians 2:4 HCSB

Snapshot

Selflessness means you think less about yourself—you consider others' needs and interests and not just your own. Circle which statement sums up Philippians 2:4:

a) Everyone should look only to their own interests, always. Who cares what someone else needs!

b) Everyone should consider the needs of others because that shows you care.

It's natural to only think of ourselves, but as we grow in our faith, we realize how important it is to love others and consider their needs too. We will grow closer to our friends as we show them we care. As we are selfless with our friends, they will also be encouraged to be selfless.

In each scenario below, circle examples of *selflessness*.

Scenario 1:

a) You need homework help, but your friend wants to play a game, so she doesn't help you.

b) You need homework help, and even though your friend was going to play a game, she stops to help you.

Scenario 2:

a) A friend is a good listener. She shares about her life but then also listens to you.

b) A friend only talks about herself the whole conversation.

Scenario 3:

a) A group of friends decides not to talk to you anymore, and the friend you're closest with also ignores you. She doesn't want to be left out.

b) When a friend group ignores you, your closest friend considers your feelings and hangs out with you, regardless of what the other girls are doing.

Friends who are selfless are thoughtful and much more fun to be friends with.

Flipside

The flipside of selflessness is selfishness, which means being consumed with oneself.

In Mark 9, Jesus and His disciples were on their way to Capernaum.

Jesus was telling them how He would die and after three days rise again. Guess what the disciples were doing as they walked along the road? They were arguing. What do you think they were arguing about?

a) They argued about how to share the gospel and reach the most people.

b) They fought over what they would have for dinner.

c) They argued about who was the greatest.

Jesus asked them what they were arguing about, even though He already knew. "But they kept quiet because on the way they had argued about who was the greatest. Sitting down, Jesus called the Twelve and said, 'Anyone who wants to be first must be the very last, and the servant of all'" (Mark 9:34-35).

Jesus had just shared about how He would have to die and rise three days later, yet the disciples were preoccupied with themselves and were most concerned about who was the best. What two actions would have been examples of selflessness in this situation?

a) They could have asked Jesus how He felt and shared His sadness.

b) They could have raced one another along the road to prove who was the best.

c) They could have asked Jesus if there was anything He needed or how they could be there for Him.

Being selfless in your friendships is a great way to show the love of Jesus to our friends.

Selflessness is an important part of good friendships.

Unwind Your Mind

? Do you tend to be selfish in your friendships? How has that affected them?

_____

_____

_____

_____

_____

_____

? What are some ways you have been selfless in your friendships, and how has that helped them?

_____

_____

_____

_____

_____

_____

What Do I Do?

"How do I get better at being selfless?"
—Ashley

Dear Ashley,

Great question. Selflessness is a quality we are all working on. It doesn't come naturally to any of us, so you're not alone. But there are some things you can do to become more selfless.

You can memorize Scripture, such as Philippians 2:4. And then watch how the Lord brings His Word to your heart in the middle of the day. You might even be in the middle of being selfish when God pops His Word into your mind.

When you're in a conversation, you can ask a friend a question about herself. Then ask her a follow-up question before you start talking about yourself. For example, you could ask your friend what she did this past weekend. If she says she went to see a movie, you could ask her which movie and what she liked about it. Then you can share about your weekend. Practicing this will help you get better at it.

Another way you can get better at it is by asking God to give you opportunities to be selfless and to love your friends well. When you catch yourself being selfish, ask God to help you be selfless and considerate of others.

And just the fact that you want to be more selfless is awesome! It's a process, so be patient with yourself. As you seek God, you will grow in selflessness.

Love, For Girls Like You

"How can I serve my friends selflessly without expecting something in return?"

—Sophia

Dear Sophia,

Serving selflessly without expecting something in return is what the Bible calls us to! That doesn't mean it's easy, though. Naturally, we want a reward or for someone to notice our good deeds. Luke 6:35, however, commands us to love our enemies and do good to them without expecting anything in return. Selfless servanthood is the heart of God. When we think of what God did for us, we are reminded that Jesus selflessly came to earth and served us! Jesus didn't receive anything in return from doing this either. He washed the feet of sinners, healed diseases, and, most importantly, died on the cross so we could spend eternity with God. Do you know what Jesus got in return? Nothing! He was mocked, brutally beaten, and crucified. Talk about selflessness. If the God of the universe serves us, how much more should we serve others selflessly? We get to follow His example and embody His nature in selfless servanthood to our friends, our families, and even our enemies.

Love, Olivia

24

Reconciliation

Soul Scripture

"Therefore, if you are offering your gift
at the altar and there remember that
your brother or sister has something
against you, leave your gift there in front
of the altar. First go and be reconciled
to them; then come and offer your gift."

Matthew 5:23-24

Snapshot

If you have reconciliation with a friend after an argument, that means you worked things out. To reconcile means to be connected again.

Imagine running a mile. Now imagine running a mile while wearing a heavy backpack. How much harder would that be? When we have something against a friend and are in an argument, it's like carrying a weight on our back because of the frustration and bitterness it can put in our hearts. Matthew 5:23-24 tells us how to get rid of that heavy weight and how to have peace instead.

The word *altar* in this verse refers to a place in the Bible where people would offer their gifts to the Lord: "Therefore, if you are offering your gift at the altar and there remember that your brother or sister has something against you, _____ your gift there in front of the altar. _____ go and be _____ to them; then come and offer your gift."

What does this Scripture say you should do?

a) You should be difficult to get along with so you can have conflicts with friends.

b) Time yourself to see how long you can stay mad at your friend.

c) First, reconcile with your friend, and then come offer your gift to God.

If someone does *a* or *b*, that person will be pretty unhappy and people won't want to be friends with them. But when someone tries to have reconciliation in friendships, they become good at staying connected to friends.

Flipside

The opposite of reconciliation is division—not the math term, though! In friendships, if there's division, there's conflict and separation. It happens when we have an unresolved argument and don't work things out. Division leads to hurt and broken friendships.

In Luke 15, Jesus told a story about division between a father and son. The son took the money his father had given him and made poor, sinful decisions. The son ended up running out of food and didn't have a place to stay. He was in desperate need and realized he messed up.

Instead of being prideful, the son decided he wanted to reconcile. He went to his father to ask for forgiveness but assumed his father wouldn't accept him back.

But while he was still a long way off, his father saw him and was filled with compassion for him; he ran to his son, threw his arms around him and kissed him. The son said to him, "Father, I have sinned against heaven and against you. I am no longer worthy to be called your son." But the father said to his ser vants, "...Let's have a feast and celebrate. For this son of mine was dead and is alive again; he was lost and is found." So they began to celebrate (Luke 15:20-24).

The son finally realized his sin and asked his father for forgiveness. This is a beautiful example of God's forgiveness for us too. We didn't do anything to deserve God's forgiveness, yet He has open arms to us when we ask Him for forgiveness.

How are we reconciled with the Lord and forgiven?

a) We are connected to God through His Son, Jesus Christ.

b) We are reconciled to God through doing enough good acts.

c) We are forgiven and connected to God by being nice.

We are reconciled, forgiven, and connected to God through His Son, Jesus Christ—what a reason to celebrate!

Remember that all close friendships have conflicts and disagreements at times, but it's important to try to have reconciliation and not division. God cares deeply about reconciliation.

Reconciliation is an important part of good friendships.

Unwind Your Mind

Has there been a time when there was conflict in one of your friendships and you didn't reconcile? How did it affect your friendship?

_____

_____

_____

_____

_____

_____

Is there a time when you had a conflict or argument with a friend and one of you tried to reconcile? What happened?

_____

_____

_____

_____

_____

_____

What Do I Do?

"What steps can I take to reconcile with a friend I've had a disagreement with?"
—Carly

Dear Carly,

It would be nice if reconciliation was easy and we could wave a magic wand and all would be well. While it takes effort and time to reconcile, it's worth it. There are some steps you can take to have reconciliation with your friend.

Before you go to your friend about what you're upset with, think about ways you could have loved her better too. When you go to her, if there's something you need to ask forgiveness for, you can start with that.

Then you can share what hurt you with a statement like, "I felt _____ when you _____." If you focus on how it hurt you and how her action made you feel, she will be less defensive than if you attack her or call her a name.

You can't control her response—all you can do is share your heart and hope you are able to work it out. At this point, it is out of your hands.

God will bless you for trying to reconcile. Leave it in His hands.

Love, For Girls Like You

"What does God say about reconciliation?"
—Rose

Dear Rose,

God knew that friendships would get messy. That's why He tells us what to do when they do. Whether we sinned against our friend or they sinned against us, *or* there's just a disagreement and no one is wrong, God urges us to reconcile.

The Bible encourages us to reconcile, always. As Christians, we should try to make peace anytime conflict arises with our friends. It's not easy, but it is worth it.

Matthew 18:15 tells us that if a friend sins against us, we should go to them in private. If you have a problem with something your friend did to you, it's important to speak to her in private. This ensures she feels respected and loved by you and keeps the situation from getting bigger than it needs to. If the situation gets worse, then it may be helpful to bring in a trusted adult or friend to help mediate.

Reconciliation requires forgiveness and humility. It doesn't mean you'll always end up agreeing, but it does mean that by taking on a posture of humility and choosing to forgive, you aid in making peace. Reconciliation isn't just good for your friend, it's good for you and your heart. A heart that reconciles is soft and at peace, and that is what you want!

Love, Camryn

Love

Soul Scripture

"Love is patient, love is kind. It does not envy, it does not boast, it is not proud. It does not dishonor others, it is not self-seeking, it is not easily angered, it keeps no record of wrongs. Love does not delight in evil but rejoices with the truth. It always protects, always trusts, always hopes, always perseveres. Love never fails."

1 Corinthians 13:4-8

Snapshot

There are so many parts to the word *love*. If you were to think of a car, it is made up of many parts that make it a car and help it run. Love is the same. So many different qualities make up the word *love*—qualities that help us love friends well.

Circle the qualities in 1 Corinthians 13:4-8 that you do well in your friendships and underline the qualities you would like to work on.

Jesus is the greatest example we have of love—taking our place and giving His life for us on the cross. Look up John 3:16 (NIV) to fill in the blanks if you don't know the answers: "For God so

_____ the world that he _____ his one and only Son, that whoever _____ in him shall not perish but have _____ life."

God loved through action. He didn't say He loved us and then not do anything to show it. In the same way, which example below shows a friend who loves?

a) Your friend doesn't spend time with you.

b) Your friend says she cares about you, but she is mean to you.

c) Your friend is kind to you, spends time with you, and uplifts you.

Putting our words into action is a big part of loving our friends. Words don't mean much if we don't follow through with showing we care. When we love one another, we are doing just what Jesus called us to do.

First John 4:11 says, "Dear friends, since God so loved us, we also ought to love one another."

So why should we love others? Because "God so _____ us."

Flipside

The flipside of love is hatred, which is intense, passionate dislike. When we have hatred for others, it hurts our hearts. However, if someone is being mean to you, it's okay to have boundaries and not be around them to protect yourself. Instead of building up hatred in your heart, you can pray for that person.

While God does not want us to hate people, something that God says we should hate is sin—ways in which we are unloving to God or one another. In the following verse, circle what we should love, and underline what we should hate: "Let those who love the LORD hate evil" (Psalm 97:10).

In Proverbs 6:16-19 there's a list of seven things God says He hates. Underline all seven of them: "There are six things the LORD hates, seven that are detestable to him: haughty eyes, a lying tongue, hands that shed innocent blood, a heart that devises wicked schemes, feet that are quick to rush into evil, a false witness who pours out lies and a person who stirs up conflict in the community."

God hates sin because it pulls us away from loving Him and loving those around us. Good friendships cannot be built on the things God hates.

Good friendships can be built on love. Just as we need to put gas into a car so it can run, we need to fill our tanks, or hearts, with love so we can have good friendships that honor the Lord.

Circle ways we can grow our friendships and fill up our hearts with love instead of hate:

a) Spend time in prayer with God.

b) Lie in small ways and be deceitful.

c) Rush into the wrong thing.

d) Spend time around people who make good choices.

e) Stir up conflict with friends through gossiping.

f) Read the Bible and memorize verses.

g) Be haughty and prideful.

h) Forgive your friend when she hurts you.

i) Do kind things for your friends.

Options *a, d, f, h,* and *i* are all great ways to grow our friendships. Proverbs 10:12 says, "Hatred stirs up conflict, but love covers over all wrongs." While hatred for people is something that leads to difficulty and hurts our hearts, love leads to God and life, and it covers everything.

Love is the most important part of good friendships.

Unwind Your Mind

? Do you struggle with something on the list in Proverbs 6:16-19? Write about it.

_____

_____

_____

_____

_____

_____

? Why do you think love is the most important part of good friendships?

_____

_____

_____

_____

_____

_____

What Do I Do?

"How can I love my friends when I don't feel like it?"

—Hannah

Dear Hannah,

This sure can be hard! There are so many times when we might not feel like loving a friend or being kind. But that's why love is a choice, not always a feeling. If we just loved others when we felt like it, then our friendships wouldn't be strong or last.

A verse that can help us with this is 1 John 4:11: "Dear friends, since God so loved us, we also ought to love one another." That is a great motivation. It can help to write this verse on your mirror with a dry erase marker and memorize it. When you don't feel like loving your friends, this verse will help.

When we choose to love our friends, over time, it will become more and more natural. We will be doing the Lord's work and what He has called us to do. And we will become more like Him.

"And now these three remain: faith, hope and love. But the greatest of these is love" (1 Corinthians 13:13). Your friendships will bloom as you and your friends love one another well.

Go love your friends well, girl. You got this!

Love, For Girls Like You

"How can I love others the way God loves them?"

—Olivia

Dear Olivia,

Beautiful question. Recognizing that God loves them is the first step to learning to love them in the same way.

John 3:16 tells us that God loves each of us so much He sent His Son to die for us. God couldn't imagine spending eternity without us, so He sent His Son to bridge the gap. Do you know how crazy that is? How great a love that shows?!

When we remember that God loves everyone, we see people differently. Rather than seeing them as just another human, we see them as God's children, which makes them our brothers and sisters.

The Bible says there is no greater love than to lay your life down for another. Loving others the way God loves them looks like sacrifice. The chances you will have to give up your literal life for your friend are slim. Think of sacrifice in friendship as servanthood. The greatest way to love is to serve.

If you want to love others the way God loves them, you must serve others the way God serves them. Look around for the needs of others and put them first. It may not come naturally at first and it definitely won't be easy, but as you spend time with God and read His words, you will learn how to love others the way He loves you and me.

Love, Alena

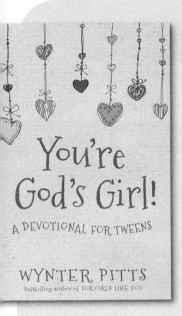

Discover the True You!

These daily devotions written directly to your heart will help you discover God's truth—who He made you to be, how unique and special you are, and how you fit into your world.

Get Creative and Colorful

Take God's amazing truths into your heart as you add color to these cool designs using your crayons, colored pencils, watercolors, or markers.

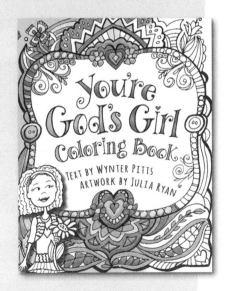

Available wherever awesome books are sold.

magazine and resources for girls

If you've wondered whether there is anything left on the planet to entertain your young beauties that promotes morals you'd approve of, look no further.

——**Priscilla Shirer**, author and speaker

A Fun & Inspiring Magazine for Young Girls

FOR GIRLS LIKE YOU is a Christ-centered, fun-filled, edutainment-style magazine created just for girls like your tween!

FOR GIRLS LIKE YOU will help you grow, teach, entertain, and inspire your daughter to be **GOD'S GIRL** first! With fun activities, interactive pages, features on God's Girls around the world and right next door, articles about people they know and love, inspiring stories on what God is doing in the world, and a whole lot more—every issue shows **GIRLS LIKE YOU** how to live as **GOD'S GIRL**.

• A break from technology • Affirms tween girls in who God created them to be • Story-driven by girls and for girls • Gospel-centered • Fun

ForGirlsLikeYou.com

FOR GIRLS ♥ like YOU

IS FOR GIRLS LIKE YOU AND BY GIRLS LIKE YOU!

Don't miss an issue! SUBSCRIBE NOW!

● Meet Girls Like You and read about the AMAZING things they are doing!

● Read YOUR stories and see your creativity in every issue!

● Super themes about the things you LOVE

● Laugh out loud at our punny LOL page!

● Awesome and easy crafts to do

● Devotionals and inspiration for living as God's Girl

● Learn a lot and have a lot of fun while you do!

Wynter Pitts' vision continues in For Girls Like You Magazine—inspiring tweens to live as God's Girls!

ORDER:

GIRLS like **YOU**

Online · By Phone · Mail This Card

ONLY $24.95 for a whole year!

Don't miss an issue!

ForGirlsLikeYou.com
888-906-9055